D0842239

Six Months to Oblivion

WERNER GIRBIG

Six Months to Oblivion

**The Eclipse of the Luftwaffe
Fighter Force**

HIPPOCRENE
BOOKS, INC.

New York, N.Y.

AUTHOR'S ACKNOWLEDGEMENTS A chronicle of this scope could not have been compiled without the help of former fighter pilots or their relatives, members of groundstaffs and administrative personnel, and last but not least the wide circle of individuals who have knowledge of the events at second hand. The details they furnished here often provided the clues with which to unravel the documentation available.

I should like to thank the following in particular for the help, support, suggestions and information which they have provided: Major Helmut Ballewski (Porz-Lind), Brigadier-General Dieter Bernhard (Munich), Emil Bischof (Garbsen), Colonel Georg Füreder (Wiesbaden), Lt Col Hans Harms (Munich), Günter Izquierdo (Hamburg), Armin Köhler (Giessen), Gerhard Kott (Neu-Isenburg), Dieter Krägeloh (Soberheim), Kurt Loll (Berlin), Siegfried Luckenbach (Karlsruhe), Eugen Lux (Offenbach/Main), Arno Paffrath (Bergisch Gladbach), Heinz Polak (Kelkheim/Ts.), Hans Ring (Munich), Friedrich Scheer (Neukirchen), Karl Schubert (Lohr/Main), Friedrich Trenz (Vienna), Heinz Wischhöfer (Regensburg), Gerrie J. Zwanenburg (Baarn/Holland).

Photographs: Bischof 2, Broeckelschen 1, DRK-Suchdienst; Eder 2, Hawker 2, Herwig 1, Col Holt 1, Imperial War Museum 5, Col Moon 2, Nauroth 2, North American 1, Polak 1, Republic 1, Robinson 2, Royal Air Force 2, Süddeutscher Verlag 1, United States Air Force 14, Waal 3, author's files 14; and 16, the origin of which cannot be traced. Sketch-maps by the author.

First published 1973
English Edition 1975

Translated by Richard Simpkin

© German Edition, Motorbuch Verlag, Stuttgart, West Germany
© English Edition, Ian Allan Ltd, 1975

Library of Congress Catalog Card Number
ISBN 0–88254–360–1

Printed in Great Britain

Contents

To all unknown fighter pilots,

To those who fought alone,
To the unnamed wingmen,
And to the commanders,

To the host of young pilots,
Never named and never credited with a victory,
Whose courage and readiness to give their lives
Was nonetheless equal to every demand made of them
In pitting themselves against the enemy's strength,

To the 'men in black' of the groundstaff,
Without whose unflagging support
These fighter pilots would never have taken the air,

And to our former enemies—
The pilots of the Mustangs, Thunderbolts and Spitfires.

Introductory Note to English Edition

Some guidance on the organisation and rank structure of the Luftwaffe of World War II may be helpful to the English-speaking reader.

Organisation

The key unit in the Luftwaffe, the unit that is on which loyalties and traditions were focussed and which formed an administrative and, where possible, an operational entity, was the *Geschwader*. This was nominally commanded by a colonel; but under the German system promotion did not automatically accompany a command appointment, and so one frequently finds lieutenant-colonels or majors in command of *Geschwadern*. Generally speaking, German commands ran one rank lower than their British and American opposites.

The *Geschwader* usually consisted of three first line *Gruppen*, with a fourth reinforcement or training *Gruppe* which often came to be employed operationally under pressure of war. Fighter *Gruppen* normally had three *Staffeln* each, and bomber, transport etc. *Gruppen*, three. Fighters usually operated individually or in pairs *Rotten,* so that there was no firmly established sub-unit within the *Staffel*; bomber *Staffeln* were subdivided into Vics of three, *Ketten*.

The higher command structure varied considerably both with the role and under pressure of events and is extremely difficult to correlate with its Allied equivalent. In fighters, the principal operational headquarters was the *Jagdkorps* within Germany or the theatre air headquarters (eg *Luftkommando West*), and tactical control was exercised from *Jagddivision* or sector HQ, *Jagdabschnitt*.

There was no unified command by role equivalent to Royal Air Force Fighter Comand, but the fighter force (as also the bomber force etc.) was represented at Luftwaffe HQ by a Director of Fighters (General der Jäger), normally of air rank.

The German custom of using arabic and Roman numerals for alternate levels is retained in the English edition – e.g. 1 *Staffel*, II *Gruppe*, 3 *Jagdgeschwader*, abbreviated in German to 1.II/JG3.

Geschwader designations always included an indication of role.

Below is a rough comparative table of German, British and US organisations. For accuracy, however, Luftwaffe nomenclature is used throughout this book.

GERMAN	BRITISH	US
Luftflotte	Air Force*	Air Force*
Jagdkorps,		Air Division,
Fliegerkorps	Group	Bombardment Division etc
Jagddivision† ⎫ *Fliegerdivision*⎭	Sub-Group	—
Geschwader	Wing	Bombardment Group, Fighter Group etc
Gruppe	Squadron	Squadron
Staffel	Flight	Flight

* As in '2nd Tactical Air Force', 'United States 8th Air Force' etc.

† In the course of the war, this level was generally replaced by the *Fliegerkorps*, being retained only ad hoc or for special operational purposes.

Ranks

To represent the German rank structure as precisely and clearly as possible this edition uses Royal Air Force nomenclature for non-commissioned ranks and United States Forces terms for officers. A comparative table follows.

German	Translation	Abbreviation
Generaloberst*	Colonel General	—
General	General	—
Generalleutnant	Lieutenant-General	—
Generalmajor	Major General	—
Oberst	Colonel	Col
Oberstleutnant	Lieutenant-Colonel	Lt Col
Major	Major	—
Hauptmann	Captain	Capt
Oberleutnant	First Lieutenant	1st Lieut
Leutnant	Lieutenant	Lieut
Oberfeldwebel†	Senior Warrant Officer	SWO
Feldwebel	Warrant Officer	WO
Unteroffizier	Sergeant	Sgt
Obergefreite	Corporal	Cpl
Gefreite	Leading Aircraftsman	LAC
Flieger	Aircraftsman	AC

* This is not a specific rank in the British or US armed forces, but equates to a 'four-star general'.

† The term 'SWO' has been used both because this rank rates rather below the British WOI and to avoid the use of Roman numerals other than in Unit designations. The "WO" rank lies, in British terms, somewhere between Warrant Officer and Flight Sergeant.

German	*Translation*	*Abbreviation*
Oberfahnrich‡	Senior Cadet	S/Cadet
Fahnrich	Cadet	—

‡ There were various categories of cadet or ensign and various ranks within those, eg Cadet-Sergeant. The two cadet ranks included are those most frequently occuring in this book.

Introduction

Many historians take the view that the decline of the German fighter force became evident as early as 1940 and 1941, as the Battle of Britain ran its course. There is of course some truth in this, for the drain on its manpower that the Luftwaffe suffered at that time must indeed have influenced the subsequent course of the war. Yet at that stage British Fighter Command was so severely battered that, had the Germans stuck to their plan of attack and concentrated exclusively on putting the enemy fighter force out of action, it too could scarcely have survived. In truth it was not until the autumn of 1944 that the German fighter force set foot down the sacrificial path; and it was the controversial *Operation Baseplate* of January 1st, 1945 that dealt this force a mortal blow and sealed its fate. What happened from then on was no more than a dying flicker.

It is this operation, which took such an apalling toll, that provides the focal point of this account. But no report on Operation Baseplate would be complete if it did not also cover the final obliteration of the fighter force.

A study of many existing publications dealing with the Luftwaffe's battle against the Allies and the heavy fighter pilot casualties in the Western Theatre and over Germany itself inevitably moots the question: 'Did the fighter pilots let the side down?'

Today we can only record how they took off time and again in face of overwhelming odds and well knowing what a slender chance they stood of getting home again. Day after day they shaped up to the packs of the Allied fighter escorts, which so outnumbered them, and took up the unequal challenge anew. To begin with Göring, not realising the true situation, may have boastfully asserted that 'his Air Force would soon fix that; but when the setbacks came he lost little time in trampling the fighter pilots underfoot with accusations of incompetence and cowardice. But was it really their fault that one city after another succumbed to the hail of bombs and that they had little to set against the enemy's material superiority bar their fighting spirit, bred of a cross between courage and desperation?

The purpose of this chronicle is not to resolve the question of blameworthiness but simply to abide by such hard facts as have emerged from the folly of that last world conflagration. In any event no distinction can be drawn between the Allied bomber crews who rained down bombs on the cities of the whole world's enemy in full conviction of the justice of their mission, and the fighter pilots who, with a like belief in the rightness of their actions, did battle against those detestable bombers. Men of both sides alike, on the one the simple sergeant with his eye to the reflex sight of a 1,400HP Messerschmitt and on the other his fellow behind the Browning machine-gun in the rear turret of a Flying Fortress, went into battle under the same orders—'to ward off and destroy the enemy.'

But scapegoats always have to be found when the plans of the high and mighty begin to go awry; and so it was that from summer 1943 onwards German fighter pilots were time and again to become the butt of harsh reproaches, to be accused of having lost mastery of the air through their own fault and of failing through personal shortcomings to exploit the superiority of their equipment. Pleas and factual reports alike from commanders right up to the level of the Director of Fighters himself simply glanced off the obstinacy and imperception of the High Command, and were frequently even dismissed as unworthy of credence. But the heavy casualties which the fighter force suffered tell rather a different story, and the real reasons for the inadequacy of our home air defence must be sought in quite different quarters.

Right from its inception the whole Luftwaffe was shaped to match an offensive strategy, and in the light of early campaigns this decision may have looked sound enough. Unfortunately, however, no one at that time devoted any thought to the course the war might subsequently take. The lessons that the bitter experiences of the Battle of Britain taught were not learned, with the result that offensive thinking remained in the ascendant. Meanwhile the enemy, having formed a correct appreciation of the likely turn of events, was able to build up a powerful strategic air capability.

By the time the High Command of the Luftwaffe realised the danger, it was already almost too late. The fighter force, suddenly thrown onto the defensive, had no choice but to spread itself out geographically in penny-packets and found itself short of manpower and equipment, while the Allies with virtually unlimited logistic resources at their disposal had no need to disperse their forces. The German side also suffered from a lack of advanced aircraft; right to the end of the war the fighter force was flying the same old types, the Me109* and the FW190, much modified and thus increasingly prone to problems. Insufficient attention was paid to aircraft production, and faulty appreciations led to new developments either being shelved in favour of other, seemingly more attractive projects while still in the experimental stage, or only reaching quantity production in face of the gravest of difficulties. Moreover on the one occasion when the opportunity existed to put into production a fighter with a performance that represented a revolutionary step forward, the machine had to be switched to a role wholly foreign to its concept.

Continued underestimation of the worth of the enemy's long-range fighters proved to be a grievous mistake which was to have disastrous consequences. Again, there was no proper coordination of the formations assigned to home air defence. Last but not least the failure to build up a realistically planned, adequate and coherent fighter command in Germany itself clearly demonstrates a gross lack of foresight in the highest quarters. All this enabled the enemy to pin

---

* Known in the Luftwaffe as the Bf 109 (Bf = Bayrische Flugzeugwerke, the former name of Messerschmitt).

down the German units stationed in the West and thus overfly Germany at greatly reduced risk.

When the war in the air took on menacing proportions, it was all too easy to lay the blame for failure at the door of the fighter pilots, who in reality were achieving extraordinary feats. But their dash, courage and fighting spirit could not of their own suffice to offset the omissions and mistakes of the Luftwaffe High Command.

In the very few instances where statements supporting the fighting men's pleas made themselves heard in high places, these were in blatant contradiction to earlier rejections of the same pleas —yet another indication of perplexity in the highest places and of their inability to coordinate the employment of the Air Force and to take logical decisions. In response to accusations that the fighter pilots lacked the will to win, Hitler had this to say at a review of the situation on November 6th, 1944:

'This proves once and for all that either the pilots or their machines are no good. We can't argue that it's the pilots, because it's they who get shot down. So it must be the machines. But I have quite the opposite view of the Luftwaffe—their aircraft are good. The whole thing's ridiculous.'

Hitler then went on to say that under the circumstances there seemed no point in making any more fighter aircraft at all.*

And the Supreme Commander of the Luftwaffe? During a tour of inspection in Berlin after a heavy raid on that city in November 1943, Göring turned to his aides with the words: 'Air raid precautions? What we need is fighters. Fighters!' In September 1944 fighter production in fact reached its peak for the whole War—2,876 Me109s and FW190s. But by this time, thanks to the grave consequences of the turn for the worse the war in the air had meanwhile taken, to our losses brought about by the enemy's superiority and inadequate training of our own pilots, and to mistakes in the deployment of air defence resources, Göring had become convinced that the fault must lie with his pilots.

In the light of our knowledge today, one more factor must be adduced to round off this *exposé* of the collapse of the German fighter force in the final phase of the war. This is done not for the sake of flinging mud at a system without a conscience, rather to take an opportunity to erect a Bauta Stone† to those who were just unknown pilots. To make the point, the key events in the air defence of Germany between the beginning of 1943 and October 1944 must be reviewed.

1943

At the turn of 1942/43 the Luftwaffe in the East had taken its hardest knock so far at Stalingrad; and in the West too, as 1943 began, the fighter force, although still claimed to be superior, was encountering an enemy whose strength was mounting steadily, and was having to face a superiority in equipment that was patently on the increase.

Then something happened which a few months earlier would have been

* The subject of this review was the heavy fighter losses sustained over Central Germany on November 2nd, 1944; see also the extract from this discussion on page 25 (Author).

† A prominent uncarved tombstone or memorial used to honour heroes of the Viking era. (Tr)

thought impossible or at least incredible—the Americans joined in the bombing offensive against Germany. As early as January 27th, with a raid on Wilhelmshaven, the US Eighth Air Force made its first daylight attack on a city in German territory. The Luftwaffe High Command attempted to reinforce the inadequate defences by using a number of night-fighter units by day. But the night-fighter crews, accustomed as they were to completely different conditions, found it difficult to adjust to the daylight role; crews with a good record of success by night were not up to their new task and took damaging losses.

On May 4th the German fighters in the West made the acquaintance of the American Thunderbolt on its first operation as escort to the heavy bombers. The target was the port of Antwerp. And from this day on the doughty P-47s provided a constant escort for the Flying Fortresses and Liberators of US Eigth Air Force. The fact that American fighters too were now operating over the Low Countries was of course realised on the German side, but its significance was not. Despite the technical data available on them, no one wanted to believe that the depth to which these American fighters could penetrate would very soon increase. Göring exploded with rage when Galland put forward the view that the Ruhr would soon come within reach of enemy fighter escort operations.

Then came the moment when the American escort fighters suddenly thrust deeper-in alongside their bombers. The Thunderbolts were carrying supplementary fuel tanks which gave them a considerably increased radius of action. Göring, however, continued to ignore this threat. In the middle of the year the US Ninth Air Force, joined later by the Fifteenth, started to launch raids on Austria and South Germany from Italy; this opened up a new front on which appropriate defences had hurriedly to be set up. And the German heartland remained as it had always been—a fortress without a roof. The fighter production programme initiated by the Head of Luftwaffe Procurement, General Milch, unfortunately failed to come up to expectations; for no account had been taken of enemy destruction of production facilities, of the loss of fuel stocks in previously occupied territories or of a difficult pilot reinforcement situation. The only hope of success lay in the concentration of fighter units in German territory proper.

To quote Galland on the escort fighter problem: 'Outside fighter escort range our pursuit and night fighter operations are successful. If we gave up any serious attempt to engage on the peripheries and pulled our fighters right back, we should, in logic, at the same time be able to use them in high concentration at key points.'

But Göring would have none of this, for he at once underestimated the enemy and had an exaggerated view of our own capabilities. So the existing concept continued unchanged. This may have been simply because the considerable numbers of enemy aircraft shot down by German day and night fighters gave cause for confidence, while against this broad background the losses so far suffered were not particularly striking and could readily be regarded as acceptable.

It is true that in late summer 1943 the Allies were still a long way from dominating German airspace; but the mounting intensity of attacks on fighter production plants presaged a major weakening of the fighter force, which would sooner or later be bound to bring about a shift in the relative strengths in German skies—in other words, the loss of German air superiority. The Luftwaffe High Command, on the other hand, shut its ears to pleas and facts alike and allowed itself to be deluded by the major local defensive successes the fighter pilots had achieved.

US 8th AF, based in England, was clearly deeply concerned at the bomber losses it was sustaining, particularly those suffered in the daylight raids on Schweinfurt and Regensburg on August 17th and October 14th, to the point indeed where mass attacks on Germany were temporarily suspended. The Allies still lacked fighters which could accompany and screen their bombers deep into the German heartland; limited radius of action meant that escorts could be provided only over short distances within the German frontiers. From that point on the bombers had to make their flight to the target and back on their own and were at full risk.

Nor did British Bomber Command escape unscathed. Night-fighter kills reached their peak in 1943, even before the battle of Berlin. On the night of August 23rd over 50 four-engined bombers were shot down, and this success was repeated on the night of September 1st when 47 British machines failed to return to base.

Dispersal of the units assigned to home air defence over numerous airfields, creating less than ideal conditions for successful operation; disregard of the fighter escort problem; and last but not least the bad weather of autumn 1943—all these factors combined to produce a striking increase in fighter casualties. In fact the bad weather itself led to substantial losses of pilots and machines, for both the requisite pilot training and even the simplest of navigation equipment were lacking.

For the first time the shortage of commanders began to make itself felt. 'It is true,' Galland observed, 'that the Luftwaffe as a whole has 60–70 thousand officers; but this same air force has never got beyond the figure of 7,000 aircrew officers.'*

Now for the first time the thoughtlessness and irresponsibility of disregarding the clearly recognisable trends the war in the air was to follow were exposed. At a time when German forces were being forced back on all fronts, giving up more and more ground and with it precious sources of raw material and at the same time having to accept bitter defeats, the Supreme Command failed to build up sufficient strength to protect Germany itself. But every time the subject of air defence was raised, Göring took care to change the subject a few minutes later.

In these circumstances the omens for the defence of Germany in 1944 were gloomy enough. It seemed as though the stockpiling of equipment, the build-up and the reorganisation that were going on in British bases, in fact the whole development of Allied air strength remained hidden from the High Command of the Luftwaffe.

---

* In the Luftwaffe of the time, fighters were normally flown by Warrant Officers or NCOs, with an officer as flight leader, and bomber crews were made up of commissioned and non-commissioned ranks in roughly even proportions. (Tr.)

1944

The operational command, *I Jagdkorps*, took a far more realistic view of the situation; in the light of the enemy's mounting strength, an intensification of his offensive operations was only to be expected for the spring.

At the beginning of the year the new escort fighter, the P-51 Mustang, arrived in England, and as early as January and February long drawn-out, wide-ranging air battles developed over North Germany. Although they were inferior to the Americans in numbers, the fighting capability of the German units sometimes sufficed to deal a painful blow, as the events of January 11th show. In a daylight raid on the Brunswick and Oschersleben aircraft plants US 8th AF lost about 60 four-engined bombers, even though this cost some 40 of our own fighters—losses which made it impossible for the fighter force to sustain this type of defensive operation, for so far that year, home air defence had received scarcely a single replacement aircraft.

In the week of February 20th–25th ('Big Week') a large scale operation was directed mainly on the German aircraft industry. Enemy losses in this week were appreciable, but the fighter force was unable to prevent a single one of the mass raids. The fact could no longer be overlooked that the ratio of kills to losses was so unfavourable as to leave no doubt that defensive operations would shortly become in some degree uneconomic.

For the night-fighters the situation looked rather better. Here the intensity of operations was considerably stepped up, to reach its peak with the shooting down of 96 British bombers in the RAF raid on Nürnberg on the night of March 31st, 1944. Despite this success our night fighters remained virtually helpless against enemy electronic countermeasures. Inadequate situation reporting, a command weakness rather than a technical problem, was another sore spot —and one of the reasons for single-engined night fighter units being disbanded during March.

Finally in April the Americans succeeded in gaining effective air superiority over German airspace. Time and again they struck hard against the aircraft industry and Luftwaffe stations. Unremitting losses imposed on the German fighter pilots a heavy physical and moral burden which inevitably affected their fighting potential.

Then in May air defence units once again had a wave of abuse flung at them; the fighter pilots were accused of cowardice. But it was in that same month of May 1944 that the fighter force was engaged in bitter fighting and achieving particularly notable results. According to the Military Statistical Bureau of the time and to I Jagdkorp's War Diary, they shot down 530 American machines for a loss of 384 aircraft, representing 10.7% of the sorties flown.

In June things were comparatively quiet over Germany, all enemy resources being focussed on the landings in Normandy. But the German fighters committed to the Western theatre had to pay a heavy price; the superiority of Allied strength was simply too great. This breathing-space did not however last long, for once the enemy troops had gained a firm footing and begun to advance, the air war over Germany flared up again.

On June 20th US 8th Air Force launched a major air offensive, this time with the fuel industry on the target list. The raids were so heavy that for the first time the damage caused in the various installations led to a sustained shortfall in production. These raids continued until, towards the end of the year, a fuel shortage had set in. This was to have a decisive effect on the whole course of the war; the time had arrived when fighters stood ready on the airfields but could not take off for lack of aviation spirit.

There can be no doubt that the appearance of good long-range fighters on the Allied side constituted a turning-point. During the year the American High Command decided to give its fighter units greater freedom of action; this represented a new tactic in the development of the war in the air, to which German day fighters had to adjust. For now the enemy fighter escorts no longer had to stick close to the bomber formations but could seize the initiative in seeking out and hunting down their attackers. 'Germany is not within range of American fighters. The bomber is our main enemy.' So the Reichsmarschall was saying as late as Autumn 1943. Thus the training of pilot reinforcements remained confined to the engagement of bombers. Once the Mustang formations dominated the airspace and adopted true offensive tactics, it was inevitable that German fighter losses should rise rapidly.

Our fighter pilots found it more and more difficult to get at the bombers. An effort was made to offset the disadvantage in strength by forming 'assault *Staffeln*', as they were known, equipped with specially armoured machines. Under this concept, the 'assault fighters' would ignore the escort and drive hard in on the bombers, penetrating the screen in close formation, while 'stand-off *Staffeln*' intercepted and pinned down the enemy fighters. Good initial results seemed to prove the proponents of this offensive tactic right and led to the establishment of further assault *Staffeln*. But in the last resort these too were unable to achieve any really decisive effect. It is true that the assault fighters were sometimes able to inflict really telling losses on the enemy; but to achieve the same kill-rate, the other fighter units had to commit at least four times as many aircraft using normal tactics. The net result was that despite local successes, losses continued to rise. On top of this US 15th Air Force based in Italy, now began to step up the frequency of its raids on Southern Germany and Austria, forcing the Luftwaffe to deploy additional fighter units in defence.

By autumn the number of kills had ceased to bear any relation to the losses. Air battles on a scale so far unimagined raged over Germany, and the enemy superiority steadily became more obvious. While the total monthly losses on the enemy side remained with few exceptions under 1% of sorties flown, equivalent figures for the German fighter force were lying between 10 and 20%. It was not difficult to calculate the point in time at which the unprofitability and futility of our operations would culminate in a fiasco.

In the middle of September, on a massive scale comparable with that of February's 'Big Week', the American and British air forces struck at the armaments industry and at communications targets of all kinds. Complementary attacks on almost every airfield in Germany were probably to be seen as preparation for the major Allied airborne operation at Arnhem which began on September 17th.

In the same period a large concentration of our own fighter units in Central Germany took place. On September 12th over 400 machines stood ready for a defensive operation, but the order for take-off was cancelled because of bad weather. Göring however did not agree with this decision and personally intervened to order the fighters into the air. This nonsensical order is said to have cost the fighter force some 10% of the machines that took part, which made the September balance-sheet look less encouraging. The fighter units engaged in home air defence shot down 307 aircraft for the loss of 371. Since however the number of Allied aircraft entering the area was 18 times greater than the number of our own sorties, the respective loss ratios were 0.7% as against 14.5%. And that looked worse than unprofitable.

At the beginning of October the aircraft strength of first-line day-fighter units in home air defence amounted to 347 serviceable machines, excluding units on conversion or refresher training. After the costly and bitter fighting in the West following the Allied landings and then during August and September over Germany, Galland, in his capacity as Director of Fighters, succeeded in gaining for his units the breathing-space that had become indispensable and was mainly devoted to bringing the day-fighter wings up to strength. By the end of October the number of serviceable aircraft had almost been doubled.

Meanwhile, the intensity of Allied air activity continued to increase, with hydrogenation plants as the priority targets, and this bombing of fuel resources still further impaired their capacity. But the major communications nodes in West Germany also stood high on the list, and the armaments industry within Germany was a third focal point for sustained attack.

In the I *Jagdkorps* area operations were almost at a standstill from units being grounded; but this gave opportunity for the squadrons to be re-equipped with new aircraft and brought up to strength with pilots. A further trend was to abandon individual attacks, which had proved useless, in favour of working in large formations; only a force equalling the enemy in numbers could hope to achieve a worthwhile measure of success. Out of this the 'Big Punch' plan was born; its aim was to establish a defensive strength of 2,000 fighters and regain air superiority. Both those goals proved unattainable.

It was thanks to Galland's unremitting efforts that, in October, after protracted hesitation, the Reichsmarschall finally arranged that, of the Me262 jet fighters coming off production, all of which had so far been allotted to the hit-and-run bomber role on Hitler's orders, every twentieth machine should be handed over to fighter units. This finally made it possible to set up at Rheine, under Major Walter Nowotny, a fighter detachment equipped with the Me262. On November 1st, 1944 the detachment had all of nine Me262s serviceable.

OPERATIONAL DAY & NIGHT
FIGHTER STATIONS
& UNITS 1. 11. 44
SERVICEABLE A/C 695 DAY FIGHTERS
"   "   633 NIGHT "

A - Under refresher training / conversion

I *Air Battles over Germany*

November 1944—The Losses Mount

In the forenoon Thursday November 2nd, 1944 two bomber formations from US 8th AF crossed the Dutch coast heading east. One, 325 heavy bombers strong, was directed onto the fuel installations at Gelsenkirchen and Castrop-Rauxel, while the other, of 650* machines, flew on towards Central Germany, its target being the Leuna hydrogenation plant about $2\frac{1}{2}$ miles southeast of Merseburg, a plant which had previously been subjected to a series of heavy raids over the preceding five months.

By this stage in the war it was no longer unusual for Allied bombers to penetrate to the Central German area, but on this occasion it was noticed that the bomber formations were surrounded by a particularly strong escort, consisting of about 600 Mustangs from 8th AF and a small number of Lightnings from 9th AF. Even before the attack proper had begun several Mustang flights appear to have spotted through a gap in the clouds an airfield occupied by German fighters. Without further ado they dived and brought fire to bear on the parked machines. It was Borkheide, where I *Gruppe*, 300 *Jagdgeschwader* was stationed; the low-level attack took place just as the Messerschmitts were standing on the runway ready to take off. In a few minutes the *Gruppe* had lost an appreciable number of machines; according to a private source, 25 Messerschmitts were totally destroyed and a further 19 damaged in this attack, but these figures appear to be on the high side. They would have meant that almost the entire *Gruppe* had been put out of action, and this is contradicted by the activities of 300 *Jagdgeschwader* in the following days and weeks. Further the *Geschwader* reported not a single personnel casualty on November 2nd. If 25 machines standing ready for take-off had been so severely shot-up as to become a total loss, at least one of the pilots must have suffered some kind of wound.

Meanwhile however nearly 500 home air defence fighters were scrambling, briefed to take on the enemy flying in over Central Germany. Apart from a few largish gaps there was 9/10 cloud cover down to 1,500 to 3,000ft over Germany, with $1\frac{1}{2}$—$2\frac{1}{2}$ miles† visibility—not exactly ideal weather for an operation of this kind. Since however there was a strong front stationary over the Rhine-Main area where 2 *Jagdgeschwader* was stationed, the *Geschwader*

* 683 according to US figures (Author).

† In the English edition, flying distances, visibility etc are given in nautical miles, and ground-to-ground distances (eg between a town and a village) in (UK) statute miles.

could not get through to the Americans, so that of the machines which took off in defence only some 300 made contact. But the German fighter force was flying into its heaviest defeat so far.

Shortly before noon US 3rd Air Division, which was controlling the whole bomber force on that day, reached the target area. It was probably the 55th Fighter Group under Major Ryan which first joined battle with the German attackers. Ryan's Fighter Group reported 19 enemy aircraft shot down and one Mustang lost. Next came US 1st Air Division, with Major Preddy's 352nd Fighter Group at its head. 352nd Group first made contact at 12.21hrs and in this engagement Capt Bryan claimed 5 kills on his own account. At its debriefing 352nd Group claimed 38 German fighters shot down, while 20th Fighter Group claimed 28 kills, of which Lt Col Montgomery himself accounted for three.

The Americans reported a total of 134 German machines destroyed, three probables and a further 25 damaged. 8th AF Fighter Command gave its losses as only eight P-51s.

On the German side the greatest success went to the two assault *Gruppen*, IV *Gruppe*, 3 *Jagdgeschwader* and II *Gruppe*, 4 *Jagdgeschwader*. With a total of 61 armoured FW 190 A-8/R2s and A-8/R6s they succeeded in shooting down 30 four-engined bombers around midday, albeit at the cost of some 30 of their own machines. Over Bitterfeld 1st Lieut Werner Gerth, flight leader of 14 (Assault) *Staffel*, 3 *Jagdgeschwader*, rammed a Boeing Flying Fortress. He even managed to bale out of his Focke-Wulf, but his parachute failed to open. 1st Lieut Gerth, Knight's Cross, died with 30 kills to his credit.

Shortly after this two of his wingmen were fatally hit over Eisleben and crashed, while Sgt Küttner was wounded for the second time and had to bale out. (The first time had been in August over the Lechtal Alps when he was caught in the fire of a Liberator he was engaging.)

As IV (Assault) *Gruppe*, 3 *Jagdgeschwader*, under Captain Mortiz landed in dribs and drabs back at Schafstädt, 15 pilots were missing. Four had been wounded and had landed by parachute; the other 11 were killed.

HQ and II (Assault) *Gruppe* of 4 *Jagdgeschwader* took off from Welzow. They climbed through the towering cumulus, reached the ordered map-squares 'Kilo Echo, Kilo Delta' in barely 20 minutes and came upon the enemy over Köthen. It is difficult to imagine how coolly the pilots tried to break through the American screen and get at the bombers. And they succeeded. While III and IV *Gruppe* of 4 *Jagdgeschwader* from Alteno and Finsterwalde with their Me. 109 G-14s took on the Mustangs, the 'battering rams'* closed the bombers. The first B-17 showed signs of being hit and a few seconds later plunged steeply earthwards with two engines on fire—a score for 1st Lieut Markhoff. Sgt Scherer also had success, his Fortress diving away just as it had scored a hit on Capt Jugel, 5 *Staffel* leader who came down with his FW-190 near Klein-Badegast.

While elements of the leading bomber units had already bombed the Leuna hydrogenation plant and the head of US 3rd Air Division was already on its way back, the follow-up bombers were just opening their bomb-doors. The Ameri-

_____
* Nickname for the armoured FW 190 of the assault *Gruppen*. (Author).

cans may have been able to ward off most of the German fighter attacks so far, but when the four-engined machines got over the target it was quite another story. Here they came under fire from *Flak* positions concentrated round Merseburg. 14 Air Defence Division* succeeded in shooting down 32 more Flying Fortresses and damaging others. Despite his wounds, Lieut Femoyer, navigator of a B 17-G of 447th Bombardment Group, managed to limp his aircraft, half-shot to pieces and almost uncontrollable, back to England, only to die of his wounds shortly after landing. He was posthumously awarded the Congressional Medal of Honour.

Still the battle raged on. The Mustangs were dominating Central German airspace, and one German machine after another went down or blew up in the air.

12 *Staffel*, 4 *Jagdgeschwader*, had three killed, among them Sgt Brüggemeier, who was shot up by a Mustang while leading at Halle-Nietleben. Sgt Jessen, of 10 *Staffel*, 4 *Geschwader*, also had to bale out, but he was one of the few German pilots who lost their machines in the operations of November 2nd and came through unwounded.

As if battle casualties on this November day were not enough, bad weather and technical limitations caused further losses.

I *Gruppe*, 400 *Jagdgeschwader*, equipped with the rocket-propelled Me163 B fighter, had been stationed since summer 1944 at Brandis, east of Leipzig. This squadron, under Capt Olejnik, had the special task of close protection of the Leuna plant and November 2nd found it in action. But things went wrong from the start. SWO Rolly in 'BQ+UJ' crashed on take-off, and SWOs Bollenrath and Straznicky were shot down; all three were killed.

27 *Jagdgeschwader* under Colonel Rödel had been split up over various fronts and now after a long gap was together again, assigned to the defence of Central Germany. From October onwards its four *Gruppe* had been stationed in Saxony, and November 2nd was at once their first major operation as a group and the darkest day in the *Geschwader's* history. They met the Americans over the Leipzig area, but the Messerschmitts could not get through to the bombers. I *Gruppe* under Capt von Eichel-Streiber, having taken off from Leutewitz in its Me 109 G-14s, was suddenly engaged near Köthen by enemy fighters in great strength and straightaway involved in bitter fighting. III and IV *Gruppen* had a similar tale to tell. II *Gruppe* under Capt Keller came off lightest with only one killed and two wounded.

Widespread skirmishing took place over Merseburg, Leipzig, Zerbst and Naumburg, and in other parts of Saxony and Thuringia. German and American fighters chased each other across the skies and clinched in bitter combat. Finally the situation reached dramatic proportions. The Germans fought desperately but the odds were too great. A continuous stream of reports of crashes, parachute descents and forced landings flowed in. Pilots were not always in a position to see the last dive of their shot-down comrades; and even when they were eyewitnesses of a crash they often looked in vain for the white silk mushroom of a parachute bringing the pilot safely to earth.

With 11 killed, I *Gruppe*, 27 *Jagdgeschwader*, probably took the heaviest

* In the German armed forces structure, AA artillery was part of the Air Force. (Tr)

punishment, 1st Lieut Winkler's 1 *Staffel* alone lost five killed over Köthen and Zerbst, while 3 *Staffel* lost two pilots whose parachutes failed to open—another of the cards stacked against the airman.

By the end of the day, 27 *Jagdgeschwader* had lost 25 pilots killed and one missing; and of the 12 pilots wounded in dogfights one died of his wounds the following day—losses amounting to 38 pilots in all for the destruction of only seven Mustangs.

A comparison of the figures reported by both sides, in so far as these are available or accessible for evaluation, shows widely differing results. This is true not only of November 2nd, 1944, and it must be said that the respective figures are very rarely an approximate match or even lie in any demonstrable relationship to one another. Thus differences between one side's kill reports and the other's losses are nothing unusual, enemy losses usually being overstated. Sometimes a kill report may lead to disappointment because the enemy's reaction, a power-dive with emergency boost for instance, is misinterpreted; and some kill reports have to be revised the next day or even weeks later. In the same way a side's own losses are frequently underquoted, especially in official announcements or communiqués.

According to German casualty reports the fighter force lost at least 98 aircraft on November 2nd, 24 of these in the assault units. I *Jagdkorps* documentation puts the figure at 120, with 30 in the assault squadrons; and the Americans, as already mentioned, reported 134 confirmed fighter kills.

The official US 8th Air Force figures gave a loss of 40 four-engined bombers in all, 26 of them from German fighters. The Americans placed particular emphasis on the use of the assault *Gruppen*, attributing a quarter of the losses to 4 *Jagdgeschwader*. The report goes on to state that 457th Bombardment Group lost nine Flying Fortresses and 91st Bombardment Group as many as 12 from the attack of a single assault flight. If this refers to IV *Gruppe*, 3 *Jagdgeschwader*, it amounts to a further 21 B-17s. This gives a total of 27 four-engined machines, and in their own reports the two assault squadrons, IV *Gruppe*, 3 *Jagdgeschwader*, and II *Gruppe*, 4 *Jagdgeschwader*, claim 30 bombers shot down against 30 of their own aircraft lost.

Since other fighter units also achieved a significant sucess, the number of bombers destroyed in air-to-air engagements amounts to around 50. There can be no doubt that the US 8th Air Force losses were higher than the 40 quoted in their Official History, for with AA artillery claiming 32 aircraft shot down, the total losses of enemy bombers would come to about 80.

Widely as these individual figures differ, a really exact comparison is impossible at the moment and will become so only 30–50 years after the end of War when the time-bar on official records lapses.

But one thing is quite clear. German fighter losses on November 2nd, 1944 were dismayingly high. In case the bare figures do not bring their severity home to the reader, it is worth mentioning by way of illustration that the fighter units deployed over Central Germany in that day had *higher* losses than for instance 27 *Jagdgeschwader* suffered in its whole 20 months in the North Africa campaign.

For the first time the whole being of the fighter force was threatened.

Fighter losses on November 2nd, 1944

Units taking part*	Killed/ Missing	Wounded	Total pers/cas	Aircraft	Locality
I./JG3	4	5	9	Me109 G-14	Aschersleben,
II./JG3	11	2	13	Me109 G-14	Dessau, Halle
			22		
I./JG4		2	2	Me109 G-14	Dessau,
III./JG4	3		3	Me109 G-10/G-14	Kothen,
IV./JG4	5	1	6	Me109 G-14	Zerbst
			11		
I./JG27	11		11	Me109 G-14	Dessau,
II./JG27	1	2	3	Me109 G-14	Kothen, Leipzig,
III./JG27	5	4	9	Me109 K-4	Leune
IV./JG27	10	5	15	Me109 G-14/K-4	Merseburg, Zerbst
			38		
I./JG400	3		3	Me163 B	Brandis, Leipzig
Assault Gruppen					
IV./JG3	11	4	15	FW190 A-8	Bitterfeld, Eisleben, Halle
II./JG4	6	3	9	FW190 AO8	Kothen, Zerbst
			24		
Total losses (Germany)	70	28	98	(incl 3 *Staffel* leaders killed and 3 wounded)	

Hitler's Reaction
November 6th—8th, 1944
In the review of the situation at Hitler's headquarters on November 6th, 1944 the events of the major air battle of four days before were discussed in some detail, albeit without getting any nearer to the real underlying reasons for the setback. But some very revealing remarks were passed, and an extract from the discussion is given below:

Hitler. I've had another look at this business—I don't know whether Reichsmarschall Göring is fully in the picture. I've taken another fresh look at the whole thing and my conclusion is that 80 machines have recently been shot down.

Büchs.† 82.

Hitler. Of those 80, 50 were shot down by fighters and 30 by AA. We'll discount the 30 for the moment. The Luftwaffe had 490 machines.

Büchs. 305!

Hitler. Right, 305 made contact. But you just said 490.

* I/JG3 = I *Gruppe*, 3 *Jagdgeschwader*, etc. (Tr)
† Military Assistant to the Chief of the *Wehrmacht* General Staff. (Author).

Büchs. No, 305. The whole fighter wing at Frankfurt failed to make contact, and of 4 *Jagdgeschwader.* . . .

Hitler. All right then, 305—it come's to the same thing. And among those, he said, an assault *Staffel* with 42 machines was committed. This assault *Staffel* shot down 30 machines on its own.

Büchs. Both assault *Gruppen.* There were two assault *Gruppen.*

Hitler. With altogether. . . ?

Büchs. With altogether 63 aircraft. 61 of those made contact.

Hitler. Right, 61.

Büchs. They shot down 30 heavy bombers.

Hitler. That leaves 20 over. If you take away these 60 machines from 305, that leaves 240. So 240 machines made 20 kills in all, and themselves lost . . . 30 in the assault *Staffel*?

Büchs. Yes, 30 in the assault flights.

Hitler. And the rest lost 90. Then we have 240 sorties with 90 lost and 20 kills altogether.

*Christian.** One other thing. The assault *Gruppe* has another *Gruppe* with it which covers it.

Hitler. I don't give a damn about that. The covering squadron must shoot too. It wasn't just bombers that were shot down—some fighters were too.

Büchs. Yes, that's clear.

Hitler. Then the result is thoroughly unsatisfactory.

Christian. The key point is still that the 30 kills by the assault *Gruppen.* . . .

Hitler. Do you have someone with you to make a planned analysis of all these things? Anyway, the Reichsmarschall isn't in the picture. When he was here just now, he had no idea that our losses were so high—these damned 'failed to return' reports confuse the whole issue.

Christian. This comes up every day.

Hitler. I want to see the whole thing properly worked out. This proves once and for all that either the pilots or their machines are no good. We can't argue that it's the pilots, because it's they who get shot down. So it must be the machines. But I have quite the opposite view of the Luftwaffe—their aircraft are good. The whole thing's ridiculous. If I try and work it out, I can't make the answer add up.

Büchs. 65 machines were originally reported missing after this operation. Up to today, 38 of these in all have been traced, and 27 are still missing. All 38 air-craft were complete write-offs; 32 people were killed and six have come back wounded or unhurt.

Hitler. It takes a bit of time to sort all this out. The other day I was given the figures for one month. But someone should have said how many sorties were flown. For a month it looks crazy. But the number of sorties is what really. . . .

Büchs. I put in the number of sorties, but the figures aren't available for the whole month.

Hitler. That's the whole point! It's minute.

Christian. But *Führer*, those are percentages.

Büchs. Führer, I'm now tracing through all these operations from the 1st

---

* Major-General Eckhard Christian, Chief of Air Staff, 1944/45. (Author)

onwards and looking specially at aircraft reported missing.

Hitler. There must be someone to go through all these things properly and set out the deductions and conclusions. It must somehow be possible to get proper conclusions. We can't just say 'Well, that's the way it is.'

Christian. *Führer*, we're drawing up planning figures and forecasts all the time—Colonel General Stumpff as Commander Air Forces Germany is responsible for this. Galland as Inspector can talk to the units. The Reichsmarschall always has at his side. . . .

Hitler. Well, all I can say is no one has ever shown me any figures of this kind.

Christian. *Führer*, I've got these tables all drawn up.

Hitler. But I've never really taken them apart. One's got to do that kind of thing for oneself.

Christian. These figures are just preliminary ones. The assault *Gruppe* shot down 30 heavy bombers.

Hitler. 30. And the AA shot down 30. That leaves 20. And these come from 260 engagements. That's a rotten result. I put in 260 fighters and get 20 kills. So if I put in 2,000, I'd get 200 kills. This means I just can't count on those machines producing any . . . and they're pouring out of the factories at the devil's own pace. They're just eating up labour and materials.

Christian. The real reason, *Führer*, is that the boys hadn't flown for ten days.

Hitler. Reasons, reasons! We're always hearing about 'reasons'.

Christian. Well, that's the way things are. By contrast the *Jagdgeschwader* that took off in bad weather in the West landed back without loss, because it's flying every day, even in bad weather. You just can't get away from it.

Hitler. I don't want to say anything against the pilots. Let's stick to the kill figures for the moment; nothing can change those. It means that with 2,600 aircraft I can expect 200 kills. In other words any hope of achieving decimation by mass tactics is right out of court. So it's nonsensical to keep on making machines just for the Luftwaffe to play numbers-games with.'

November 1944 was to be the month of the 'Big Punch', the simultaneous commitment of all the fighter units concentrated in Germany. But the air battle of November 2nd put paid to this; a large proportion of the units which had been grounded for some three weeks were put in and wiped out. Analysis of the results of the day's fighting left no doubt that the planned mass operation was, for the time being at least, quite out of the question. And since the success of an operation of this kind would in any case be dependent on the weather, Hitler, who was by now convinced that his own fighter aircraft were inferior to the enemy's on every count, decided to engage with small forces too if the enemy should come in with similar numbers.

Meanwhile on November 7th Göring had issued the following edict to 'his fighter boys':

'For months now the Army has been heavily engaged in decisive battles whose outcome spells victory or defeat. The Luftwaffe has failed to meet the demands made on it.

'Comrades, our time is up! Now we must go to it and show the world that we can forge the German fighter force anew—stronger and fuller of fighting spirit and resolve than ever. Now we must prove that the hopes of the German people have not been unfounded, and that the German workman has not toiled in vain.

'Fighter pilots, it's up to you! The major fighter operation that lies before us must be the hour when a new Luftwaffe, stronger and full of victories, is born.'

If the words of this exhortation are anything to go by, the Supreme Commander of the Luftwaffe simply does not seem to have taken in the events of November 2nd.

In the meantime the 'Nowotny Trials Detachment' was forming at Achmer and early in the month flew its first operational missions. It was hardly in a position however to forge the Messerschmitt 262 jet fighter into a decisive weapon, first because low production figures meant that the Me262 was only trickling through to first-line units and second because the bulk of them were still being allocated to bomber wings.

On November 8th Major Walter Nowotny and his unit scrambled against an incursion by heavy bombers. They made an immediate interception and fought the whole of their action above the clouds. Lieut Schall, Knight's Cross, brought down three Mustang escort fighters, and Nowotny himself had just reported his third kill. But then suddenly the men down in ground control heard his desperate calls. Something was wrong with one of the jet-engines. Seconds later, the Me262 plunged out of the clouds to explode in a meadow outside the hamlet of Epe, near Bramsche. Nowotny, holder of the Knights Cross with Diamonds and with 258 kills to his credit, was dead. The actual cause of the crash was never established.

This was also to be the last operation from Achmer, for the trials detachment with its Me262s moved to Lechfeld, where it was later to form the nucleus of the new 7 *Jagdgeschwader*.

No Answer to the Mustang
Tuesday, November 21st, 1944

On November 21st 8th Air Force bombers, escorted by some 650 Mustangs, again flew in over Central Germany, following the same path as they had on November 2nd. The weather was absolutely wretched. It was raining heavily in places, the whole sky was overcast and the lower and middle layers of this cloud were thick enough to provide about 8/10 cover. Only at ground level was visibility more than 3 miles.

At their various airfields some 400 machines of I *Jagdkorps* had been waiting for some time, some of them at cockpit readiness. But the order to scramble did not come, and only a few knew the real reason for this. It had been clear since winter 1943 that foul-weather operations were barely feasible; in the day-fighter force the aircraft lacked the requisite radio installations and take-off and landing aids, and the pilots lacked the necessary training. In November 1944, a year later, only two *Geschwader* were capable of operating under these conditions. These were the bad-weather *Jagdgeschwadern* 300 and 301 *Geschwadern*, both formed from the erstwhile single-engined night fighter force codenamed Wild Boar. 300 *Geschwader Gruppen* were stationed in the Brandenburg area south of Berlin, and 300 *Geschwader* in the area Salzwedel —Sachau—Stendal.

Further, Headquarters I *Jagdkorps* tended to be hesitant to commit its aircraft in bad weather as it was anxious to avoid wasting pilots in a type of operation for which they were still ill-prepared. This is what happened on November 21st.

There was little doubt about the Americans' target for that day; the flight path pointed to another raid on Merseburg. With a severe storm front stationary over West Germany, the Germans reckoned on the likelihood of the bomber formations turning back. But the Americans pressed on and set about breaking through the storm front in the Hanover area. Only at this point did *Luftflotte*, Germany pass the order to engage to the individual *Jagddivision*.

In any event they took off too late, and the American bombers had been over the target area for some time when the fighters got there. First contact took place in cloud, when the strong enemy escort took the bulk of German aircraft by surprise while they were still forming up. It appears to have been the three *Gruppe* of 301 *Jagdgeschwader*, with their Focke-Wulf FW 190 A-9/R 11s,* which first engaged the stream of bombers. The encounter with the Mustangs of 352nd and 359th Fighter Groups had been so sudden that the Germans scarcely had time to drop their jettison-tanks. The unequal battle, fought in cloud and rain, was soon over.

301 *Jagdgeschwader* reported ten pilots killed and two missing. A further eight were wounded, three of them having baled out.

Meanwhile I and IV *Gruppen* of 300 *Geschwader* had scrambled from Borkheide and Reinsdorf. They met the Mustangs in the Hanover-Brunswick area. I *Gruppe* lost two aircraft in this operation without enemy action. Over Hildesheim a Focke-Wulf, probably from 2 *Staffel*, 1 *Jagdgeschwader*, rammed Sgt Horstkötter's Me 109; and a second Messerschmitt, Sgt Hennersdorf's 'White 8', was unfortunately shot down by our own anti-aircraft fire.

I *Gruppe*, 1 *Jagdgeschwader*, took off from Greifswald, where it had been in refresher training since the beginning of October, and headed south, guided by ground radio, to meet the bomber force over Thuringia. But the *Geschwader* must have taken the heaviest losses of any German formation that day, for the one *Gruppe* which took part in the operation was virtually wiped out. At least 20 aircraft went down, eight of them over Erfurt alone. That was two thirds of the *Gruppe* entire holding. For these pilots November 21st was their first operational mission for some time—and for many it was also to be the last.

The American bombers had long since reached the Leuna plant and almost without hindrance dropped their 475 tons of bombs on the fuel installations. Here it was only 4 *Jagdgeschwader* which tried to get its III *Gruppe* through to the bombers; but it was no more successful than 1 *Geschwader* had been in splitting open the Mustang screen. Its losses however, one killed and three wounded, were not excessive.

When the order to scramble reached II *Gruppe*, 27 *Jagdgeschwader* and IV

---

* The R 11 equipment on the FW 190 included the fire direction radio, Wireless Set 125, and was mainly fitted on the machines of the bad-weather units. (Author).

Gruppe, 54 *Jagdgeschwader* (which was under command of 27 *Geschwader*) at Hopsten, the Americans were already well on their way home. The German fighter formations made contact with the returning bombers over the Ruhr, only to get a prompt hot reception from the fighter escorts, this time Thunderbolts of 366th Fighter Group, US 9th Air Force. In engagements over the Cologne-Düsseldorf area the Thunderbolt pilots reported ten machines shot down and three probables. By contrast the II *Gruppe*, 27 *Jagdgeschwader* diary gives only five losses. However IV *Gruppe*, 54 *Geschwader* lost five Focke-Wulfs, among them the two FW 190s which crashed after colliding over Münster-Handorf.

Fighter losses on November 21st, 1944

Units taking part	Killed/ Missing	Wounded	Total pers/cas	Aircraft ·	Locality
I./JG1	15	5	20	FW190 A-8	Eisleben, Erfurt, Gardelegen, Weimar
III./JG2	1		1	FW190 A-8	Rhine-Main
III./JG4	1	3	4	Me109 G-14/K-4	Osterhausen, Querfurt
II./JG27	4	1	5	Me109 G-14/K-4	Cologne, Monchen-Gladbach, Neuss
IV./JG54	2	3	5	FW190 A-8	Krefeld, Munster-Handorf
I./JG300	2	1	3	Me109 G-14	Braunschweig,
IV./JG300	3	1	4	Me109 G-10/G-14	Gifthorn,
			7		
					Hanover, Hildesheim
I./JG301	8	4	12	FW190 A-9/R 11	Eisenach, Erfurt,
II./JG301	4	3	7	FW190 A-9/R 11	Gotha, Jena,
III./JG301		1	1	FW190 A-8	Koenitz, Stendal, Zeitz
			20		
Total losses (Germany)	40	22	62	(incl 1 *Gruppe* commander killed, 2 *Staffel* leaders killed, 1 *Staffel* leader wounded)	

There is no question but that the day's entire defensive operation must be seen as a total failure. Attacks were broken up or frustrated before they had begun. The enemy fighter escorts succeeded in involving the German fighter force in dogfights to the point of inhibiting the real business of the day, a breakthrough to the bombers. On November 21st the German fighter force lost at least 61 aircraft against only five Flying Fortresses and two Mustangs shot down—a heavy toll in blood for the fighter pilots to pay. But so many of these pilots lacked adequate operational experience that their actions had ceased to bear comparison with the proud fighter tradition that had seen the war in. The situation as a whole had long since prevented more comprehensive training, and young students from the flying and fighter schools were being posted to first-line units almost before they had mastered circuits and bumps with the Me109, to find themselves, sometimes on their very first operation, swept up in the maelstrom of a dogfight from which there was no escape. The fighter pilots were now having to pay a ridiculous price for the failure to make timely and continuous preparations for a defensive strategy.

The Fighters Hit Back
November 26th, 1944
The American offensive astride the Vosges had begun on November 14th. After bitter fighting 3rd US Army under General Patton took the ancient fortress of Metz on November 20th, and three days later occupied Strasbourg. The opponents of the German fighter units which were flung into the Lorraine battle were the strong fighter elements of 9th US TAF,* which was supporting the ground forces. Whenever the weather allowed, the American Thunderbolts were constantly over the front, with the result that dogfights constantly developed, for the most part over Hagenau Forest.

At the end of October 1944 a new unit, IV *Gruppe*, 4 *Jagdgeschwader*, was formed from elements of II and III *Gruppen*, 5 *Jagdgeschwader*. This *Gruppe*, which had taken its first losses in the fighting on November 2nd, now prepared to move from Fürstenwalde to Rhine-Main.

'*25.11.44.* First operation from Rhine-Main and five pilots lost. We were attacked by P-47s in strength while flying cover for our own troops in the Strasbourg area and South of Hagenau Forest.

Jupp Kunz's 13 *Staffel* lost Sgt Mehrens wounded and WO Lautenschläger killed near Iffezheim. 14 *Staffel* also lost 1 wounded and 1 killed—Sgt Blumenberg landed by parachute near Neuweiler and Sgt Müller was shot down by P-47s near Rastatt. In 16 *Staffel* Sgt Bintriem was wounded and baled out near Strasbourg.

Commander 4 *Jagdgeschwader*, Major Michalski, was awarded his Oak Leaves.'†

As the crews of 491 Bombardment Group left the briefing hut next day no one among them had any idea that this flight over Germany was to cost their Group extremely dear. 491 Group's Liberators took off from North Pickenham at midday. The US 8th Air Force formations assembled over southeast England, forming several waves, and headed off across the Channel for the Continent—an armada of about 1,000 aircraft. Their target was the Misburg hydrogenation plant near Hanover.

The storm front which had been stationary over West Germany a week earlier had long since moved on, and this time the Americans found the skies over Hanover almost cloudless. It was not only for 491st Liberator Group that fate lay in wait, but for their immediate opponents too. For November 26th was to be the black day of 301 *Jagdgeschwader*.

The weather conditions were now more suitable for a counter-attack, and the Germans on their side lost no time in preparing the bulk of their serviceable air-

* Tactical Air Force (Tr)
† Oak Leaves to the Knight's Cross of the Iron Cross. (Tr)

craft—some 550 fighters in all from I *Jagdkorps* and Luftwaffe Headquarters West. In the event about a quarter of these would fail to make contact with the enemy.

Meanwhile the bomber waves had passed Oldenburg in the north and were heading southeast towards the Elbe. The *Gruppen* of 1 and 6 *Jagdgeschwader* scrambled from Mecklenburg, and 301 *Jagdgeschwader* was brought to readiness on its airfields between Stendal and Salzwedel.

Long-range visibility was relatively good. The Americans' vapour trails were soon to be seen and the air defence fighters were able to set up their attack in good time. Guidance from ground control was almost superfluous this time; no one could miss the enemy's tight-packed 'combat boxes'. A force of some 50–80 machines from III *Gruppe*, 1 *Geschwader*, went in against the bomber formations on a broad front between Uelzen and Perleberg; but the Mustang escort was on its guard and had already formed up to ward them off, with the result that II *Gruppe*, 1 *Geschwader*, alone lost five fighters in as many minutes.

At this point the bomber formations, now over Wittenberge, changed heading and turned south. Then they flew west past Stendal to cross the high ground at Gardelegen and run in on the target from the east.

Meanwhile three pilots from 6 *Jagdgeschwader* had baled out near Salzwedel, all of them escaping with wounds. But it was 9 *Staffel*, with four pilots lost, that took the heaviest casualties in the squadron.

It was however only with the entry of 301 *Jagdgeschwader* that the real drama began. On November 26th all three *Gruppen* took off from the fields at Salzwedel, Sachau, Stendal and Solpke. At this moment the leading American squadrons were already just in front of Hanover, but 301 *Geschwader* formations moved in swiftly and it was just to the south of the line Brunswick-Hanover that the fateful encounter with the enemy escort fighters took place. But this time the Germans found a few gaps which allowed them to get through to the bombers, and they soon had 491 Bombardment Group's Liberators in their sights.

Suddenly the air was full of the rattle of machine-guns. Engines screamed. The first FW 190s plunged downwards, two at Mellendorf and one near Bad Münder, killing Gefreiters Henning and Dossmann and WO Handel. Over Rethen 1st Lieut Vollert, 5 *Staffel* leader, was sitting hard on the tail of a Liberator; but the two Mustangs chasing him were too quick for him, and after a wild dogfight Vollert's A-9 went down.

All this time 301 *Geschwader* was pressing home its attacks against the four-engined bombers and at the same time trying to ward off the horde of Mustangs. The escort, having let its screen be penetrated in places, now for the first time really seemed to wake up and redouble its efforts to intercept the German fighter attacks. The combat in the skies over Hanover grew more and more intense.

At the end of the day 301 *Jagdgeschwader* had 26 killed or missing and 13 wounded. Fritz Yung, who had been shot down and severely wounded over Erding at the end of April 1944, rejoined 301 *Geschwader* on his recovery. His first duty was to lay his comrades killed on November 26th to rest in the Wunstorf War Cemetery. This was a sad task for Yung, and many pilots remain

Above: In mid-1944 the newly formed 'assault *Geschwadern*' of the fighter force succeeded in achieving an above-average success rate and thus gave a fresh impulse to home air defence. The picture shows members of 10 (Assault) *Staffel*, 3 *Jagdgeschwader* gathered round their *Staffel* leader, 1st Lieut Weik (back to camera) at Illesheim in July 1944.

Below: A Focke-Wulf FW 190 A-8 of II *Gruppe*, 1 *Jagdgeschwader*, just after take-off.

Enemy bomber forces
have been reported. Day-
fighter pilots at cockpit
readiness and about to
scramble. Here the pilots
must rely on their trusty
mechanics.

Above: A pair of Me 109Gs from I *Gruppe*, 27 *Jagdgeschwader*, scrambles.

Below: From other airfields too Messerschmitts are taking off in defence against heavy bomber formations.

Above: Boeing B 17G Flying Fortresses of 447th Bombardment Group, US 8th Air Force. Almost every day German fighters repeatedly took on these American bombers in close formation in their efforts to ward off attacks on Germany.

Below: An FW 190 D-9, attacking through a bomber formation, only just avoids the falling bombs from a 4-engined machine.

Above left: Time and again our fighters broke through the barrier of American fighter escorts to get at the bomber packs. This shows the giant tail unit of a B 17G from 384th Bombardment Group which was shot down and made a forced landing.

Above right: Vapour trails in the blue sky depict the course of bitter air combat between German fighters and the intruding enemy.

Right: Flames streaming from it, an American bomber plunges downwards. This time a score for the AA gunners at Merseburg, Central Germany, on November 2nd, 1944.

Below: Photographed from the nose window of a Flying Fortress, a pair of Messerschmitts dives clear after a frontal attack on an American bomber formation.

Below: Landing after combat. On the airfields the return of the Messerschmitts and Focke-Wulfs from operations is eagerly awaited. But lack of fuel, technical faults or battle damage forced not a few machines to land elsewhere.

Above/Below: From the summer of 1944 onwards Allied air superiority
mounted steadily. Our own losses in air defence rose from week to week and sad
pictures like these became a daily event. Often there is only a tiny crater to
mark the end of a fighter pilot and his machine.

Above/Below: No account of fighter operations would be complete without a mention of the groundstaff, the 'men in black', for without them the best of fighter pilots would never have achieved success. But, thanks to the tireless work of the mechanics, even the greenest young pilot soon gained confidence in his machine.

Above/Below: Thunderbolts. This American aircraft was the heaviest single-engined fighter to be built in World War II. It was used in the European Theatre as a fighter-bomber by 9th US TAF, while the fighter units of US 8th Air Force were steadily being converted to the Mustang. Its 6–8 0.5in (12.7mm) Browning machine-guns gave the Thunderbolt massive fire power under which many a German fighter met its end.

The Royal Air Force's red, white and blue cockade on the rudder spells danger!
From autumn 1944 2nd TAF, equipped with the three types of aircraft shown
above (Spitfire IX, Typhoon IB and Tempest V) was flying almost daily
operations over North Germany to draw the German Air Force to battle.

Above: Three pilots of III *Gruppe*, 3 (Udet) *Jagdgeschwader*, safely returned to base, are given a first quick debriefing by their squadron commander, Capt Dahl.

Below: With the introduction of the FW190 D-9 yet another new type came off the production-line into first-line units. Pilots considered this aircraft, second only to the Me262, the best that the Luftwaffe had to offer. The D-9s climb rate and top speed of almost 380 knots made it a match for, and in some respects superior to all types of enemy fighter.

German fighter stations were one of the top priorities on the Allies' target lists. The photograph shows Twenthe airfield after a raid in mid-November 1944. At the turn of 1944/45 I *Gruppe*, 1 *Jagdgeschwader* as well as various night-fighter units were based there.

Above: A German *Jagdstaffel* in autumn 1944. II *Staffel*, 53 *Jagdgeschwader*, probably taken at Kirrlach. The flight leader, Lieut Landt, is sitting on the Me 109 G-14. Of the eight senior NCOs standing, three had been killed and three wounded by mid-March 1945.

Below: SWO Heinrich Bartels, killed in action on December 23rd, 1944. With 99 victories to his credit, Bartels was a veritable mentor to the young pilots of IV (Reinforcement) *Gruppe*, 27 *Jagdgeschwader*. He used to pass on his experience in a way that quickly instilled confidence.

The camera-gun of a Mustang captures the shooting down of a Messerschmitt Me109 G. In the Ardennes offensive the German fighter force took unimaginably heavy losses. In the five days from December 23rd–27th, 1944 over 260 pilots were killed, captured or reported missing.

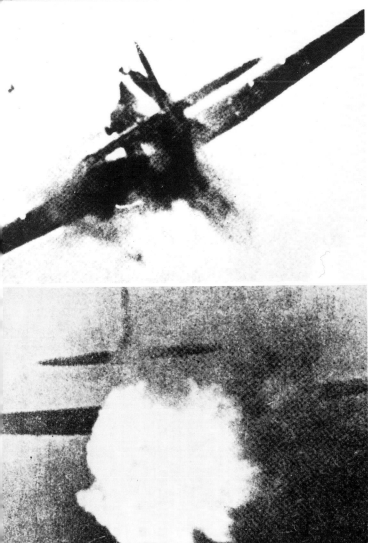

Above left: Lt Col Bühligen, the last commander of 2 (Richthofen)
Jagdgeschwader, is one of the few German fighter pilots to have marked up
over 100 kills against the Allies in the West. The photograph shows Bühligen at
Cherbourg in 1943, when he was commanding II *Gruppe*, 2 *Jagdgeschwader*.

Above right: As the scale of bombing raids on Germany steadily mounted and
our air defence failed to come up with the hoped-for successes, reproaches of
cowardice on the part of fighter pilots began to make themselves heard in the
highest Luftwaffe circles. In his capacity as Director of Fighters, Lieut-General
Galland firmly stood up for his pilots, to the point where his sharp criticisms led
to his falling out of favour and being relieved of his appointment. Only in the
last few weeks of the war—far too late—was he allowed to set up a special jet-
fighter unit, 'Fighter Formation 44'. This brought local successes, but they
came too late to have any significant influence on the course of events.

Below: Lt Col Michalski, shown here in his early days as a lieutenant with 4
Staffel, 53 *Jagdgeschwader*, commanded 4 *Jagdgeschwader* and led it against
the Belgian airfield of Le Culot on New Year's Day, 1945. The attack went
awry and the unit suffered the heaviest rate of pilot losses of the day.

unidentified to this day.

But the battle was not yet over. Having dropped a total of 862 tons of bombs on Hanover and turned for home, the American bombers reached the area of 27 *Jagdgeschwader* and IV *Gruppe*, 54 *Geschwader*, by now airborne after scrambling from Rheine, Hopsten, Achmer and Hesepe, and Vörden respectively. These units, operating under command 3 *Jagddivision* were waiting for the enemy over the Teutoburger Wald and the Ems; but 27 *Geschwader* was once again to taste the fury of the Mustangs' counter-attacks.

The first Messerschmitts shattered as they hit the ground in the flatlands astride the Mittelland Canal; and to the North, almost above their own airfield, the parachutes began to plume. More skirmishes developed in the skies round Osnabrück and spread out northwards as far as Vechta and Bersenbrück. III and IV *Grappen*, 27 *Jagdgeschwader* each lost three pilots killed, and Sgt Gerd Schmidt was reported missing. IV *Gruppe*, 54 *Geschwader*, suffered a particularly tragic loss when 1st Lieut Heinz Sterr, Knight's Cross, was shot down by a Mustang over Vörden airfield when coming in to land. Sterr had a tally of 130 kills, 127 of them in the east; he had joined 16 *Staffel*, 54 *Geschwader*, as *Staffel* leader only in the autumn of 1944, and his death cost the Squadron one of its more distinguished pilots.

Capt Haase, commanding I *Gruppe*, Udet *Geschwader* (3(Udet) *Jagdgeschwader*), was accidentally killed. The *Geschwader* had received no orders for this operation, but the unit command vic had been scrambled. Shortly after takeoff, Capt Haase collided with his wingman's machine over Erkelenz and crashed to his death.

The operations of November 26th added up to yet another painful blow for the home air defence fighters. The *Gruppen* taking part lost at least 90 machines, a figure for once not far different from the Allied claims. 339th US Fighter Group reported 29 kills, Lieut Daniel alone accounting for five FW 190s. 361st Group (Capt Duncan) claimed 19 kills, and 356th Mustang Group (Lt Col Baccus) 23. Together with a figure of 27 for 355th Fighter Group this amounted in all to 98 German fighters destroyed.

I Jagdkorps announced 35 four-engined bombers shot down, but at 20 the US 8th Air Force figures were far lower—15 Liberators from 491st Group, mentioned earlier, and five Liberators from 445th Bombardment Group.

The losses suffered up to this point had already made a mockery of continued talk of 'home air defence'. However the commanding officers, or at least most of them, might strive to use their alertness and their experience to produce at least some slight improvement in their men's slender chance of survival, the final decline of the German fighter force was under way. Perhaps the Luftwaffe High Command thought otherwise; at least they did all they could to conceal this tragedy from the public. Thus it was that the Armed Forces communiqué for the 'black 26th' contained only a brief paragraph:

'Anglo-American terror bombers penetrated by day to Northwest and Central Germany with strong fighter escort, dropping their bombs mainly in urban residential areas and on rural communities. Damage was particularly extensive at Hanover, recently the target of repeated enemy air-raids, and in Hamm.'

Fighter losses on November 26th, 1944

Units taking part	Killed/ Missing	Wounded	Total pers/cas	Aircraft	Locality
I./JG1	2		2	FW190 A-8/A-9	Helmstedt, Perleherg, Salzwedel,
II./JG1	9	3	12	FW190 A-8/A-9	Uelzen
			14		
III./JG6	6	6	12	Me109 G-14	Salzwedel, Wittstock
III./JG26	1	1	1	Me109 G-14	Oldenburg
I./JG27	2		2	Me109 G-14	Bersenbruck,
II./JG27	2	4	6	Me109 G-10/G-14	Hesepe, Munster,
III./JG27	4	2	6	Me109 K-4	Osnabruck
IV./JG27	3	1	4	Me109 G-10/G-14	
			18		
IV./JG54	2		2	FW190 A-8	Vechta, Vorden
I./JG301	13	3	16	FW190 A-9/R 11	Brunswick
II./JG301	9	6	15	FW190 A-9/R 11	Eimbeckhausen,
III./JG301	4	4	8	FW190 A-8	Hamlin, Hildesheim,
			39		Wunstorf
Total losses (Germany)	57	30	87	(including 5 *Staffel* leaders killed, 1 *Staffel* leader wounded)	

Lambs to the Slaughter
November 27th, 1944

The fine weather of the day before had changed. It is true that no rain was forecast, and visibility remained excellent; but cloud was forming and was later to give 4/10 to 6/10 cover. It was also a good deal colder.

Once again the observation posts reported Allied bomber formations airborne and forming up over the British Isles. It would not be long before General Doolittle's 8th Air Force formation set course for Germany. Sure enough, at 1100 the leading bomber wave was over the Channel, and an hour later the Americans were spread out on a broad front over the Ruhr.

The enemy was bound for communications targets in the Rhine-Main area, and was to reach them unmolested by the German defence. For strong forces of Mustangs and Thunderbolts in their hordes put a ring round the attacking waves, now flying alongside the bombers, now thrusting out ahead to spring upon the German fighters in good time. Far to the north and the east the Allied fighters threw out a screen which proved quite impenetrable. While the Fortresses and Liberators were starting their bombing-runs, fierce air fighting was in progress over Münsterland and the Harz.

At Fürstenau airfield, some 15 miles east of Lingen, I *Gruppen*, 26 ('*Schlage-*

ter') *Jagdgeschwader*, had all of six Focke-Wulfs serviceable and standing ready on the runways; but only four took part. The Messerschmitts of III *Gruppe*, 26 *Jagdgeschwader*, were scrambled from Plantlünne, and III and IV *Gruppe* of 27 *Geschwader* were in the thick of it again. Their operational area was right on their doorstep, for the American fighter formations had already penetrated to the general area Rheine-Osnabrück-Gütersloh-Münster. The party was on.

Along with the boys from 27 *Geschwader*, a round dozen machines of IV *Gruppe*, 54 *Geschwader*, took off from Vörden and headed southwest. Seconds after they were airborne and still in sight of the field, pilots and groundstaff alike were horrified to see a Focke-Wulf, apparently with engine-failure, lose height and go straight in, killing its pilot.

Between Bramsche and Bersenbrück 1st Lieut Kohl with 11 *Staffel*, 27 *Geschwader*, found himself hard pressed; the pilots had scarcely had time to bring their Messerschmitts to combat height after their take-off from Hesepe before the enemy fighters were upon them. An unending stream of Allied machines seemed to pour from the sky, and not one pilot managed to catch even a glimpse of a bomber's silhouette. They simply could not force their way through to the bombers.

As the wild hunt with its bitter infighting swept on to the north of Bramsche, individual machines could escape the deadly enemy fire only by going down to hedgetop height. It was just after midday. By this time III *Gruppe*, 27 *Geschwader* had already lost three pilots.

It was hardly surprising that, in the massed dogfights of those times, pilots were taking friend for foe and *vice versa*. Thus in the heat of battle two warrant officers of 13 *Staffel*, 27 *Geschwader*, took each other on and shot each other down. One Messerschmitt crashed in a wood near Ascheloh and the other came down not far from it in a field at Werther. Luckily both pilots, although wounded, succeeded in baling out. History does not relate what Capt Dudeck had to say about this incident at the debriefing. The same thing happened with the Americans. A Mustang pilot from 353rd Fighter Group took another machine in his own unit for a Messerschmitt and duly despatched it; and Major Juntilla, commanding 353rd Fighter Group, narrowly escaped the same fate. Nevertheless Juntilla's unit reported 21 kills that day.

Meanwhile the American fighter screens were fanning out over the Harz and the Göttingen area. The Americans knew exactly where the individual fighter units of the German home air defence were stationed, and they were expecting another intervention from 300 and 301 *Jagdgeschwader* based south and west of Berlin. To nip this plan in the bud, the US 8th Air Force fighters pressed way out ahead—a tactic which was once again to pay dividends.

II *Gruppe*, 300 *Jagdgeschwader*, stationed at Löbnitz, under Major Peters, an assault unit set up on the proven model, was already airborne and had assembled with the *Geschwader's* other three *Gruppen*, based at Borkheide, Jüterbog and Reinsdorf, to form a large tactical grouping, which two *Gruppen* from 301 *Jagdgeschwader* were also to join.

301 *Jagdgeschwader*, based in the Altmark, also was already airborne and was heading south over Brunswick to be guided on to the American formations.

Directed onto the same target, 300 *Geschwader* was flying westwards over the Brandenburg area and thence over Saxony. These fighters did not get far; for both *Geschwader* the Harz, or more precisely the area Salzgitter-Eschwege was the limit of their flight. There the Americans were already in wait for them, and the Mustangs, streaming in from all directions, went over to the attack.

It speaks well for the courage of the individual German pilots that they were able here and there, in dashing counter-actions, to press their numerically superior pursuers hard. Pushing their aircraft to the limits of manoeuvrability and beyond, they strove to get into favourable attack positions; but usually they failed and the pilot had to use all his skill to escape in one piece. The sky was full of well-trained enemy, and on the German side there were too few fighter pilots with the experience called for by an all-in dogfight. At this stage many pilots quite simply lacked the training for this type of operation. In the heat of the moment they would often forget to push over the safety-catch on the control column and press their thumbs sore until they became resigned to the fact that they could not get a single shot off and were thus defenceless. For the first time they were seeing the gruesome downward plunge of a friend who had managed to jump clear of his blazing 'crate' only to find that his parachute would not open. For the first time they were confronted with death, with the reality of war. And then it happened. While the novice, fresh from flying school, was trying to grasp all these incomprehensible things and was staring wide-eyed at machines dropping out of the sky beside him and exploding as they hit the ground, he too, paralysed by what he had seen, fell prey to the Mustangs.

The bitterest fighting raged between the Harz and the Solling Hills. 1 *Staffel* lost two pilots at Alfeld on the Leine. With six killed and three wounded in I *Gruppe*, as well as three killed in II *Gruppe*, 301 *Jagdgeschwader* had taken another hard knock; like 27 *Geschwader* it had been virtually decimated within a few minutes. The number of machines remaining serviceable fell hideously low; and the pilot reinforcements needed to bring the *Geschwader* up to strength did not exist.

Over the Harz and to the east and south the whole of Lt Col Dahl's 300 *Geschwader* became involved with enemy fighters. Once again the casualty reports piled up at *Jagdkorps* Operations Centre in Treuenbrietzen. All hell was let loose. It was the assault *Gruppe* that took the highest casualties, with two killed and two wounded in 5 *Staffel*, two killed in 6 *Staffel*, two killed and two wounded in 7 *Staffel* and one killed in 8 *Staffel*. This *Gruppe* met the enemy over the eastern slopes of the Harz, in the triangle Halberstadt-Quedlinburg-Aschersleben. In a bitterly contested action they shot down several Mustangs, but at high cost.

The outcome of the defensive operations of November 27th was catastrophic. I *Jagdkorps* took on the intrusion by US 8th Air Force with some 750 fighters, the strongest force it had yet fielded; but the American fighters succeeded in pinning down the German defence to the point where not a single bomber was destroyed. And against our own losses of over 50, only 11 Mustangs were shot down. The American fighter units—mainly 353rd and 357th Fighter Groups, the latter led by Major Broadhead—claimed 98 German fighters. Although it had by this time become very difficult to establish exact figures for German losses in home air defence, this figure seems on the high side. It is however not known whether fighters destroyed on the ground or accounted for in other ways are included.

Fighter losses on November 27th, 1944

Units taking part	Killed/ Missing	Wounded	Total pers/cas	Aircraft	Locality
I./JG26		1	1	FW190 A-8	Iburg, Osnabruck,
III./JG26	2	2	4	Me109 G-14/K-4	Munster, Rheine
			5		
III./JG27	3		3	Me109 K-4	Bersenbruck,
IV./JG27	2	2	4	Me109 G-10/G-14	Munster, Werther
			7		
IV./JG54	3	1	4	FW190 A-8/A-9	Diepholz, Ibbenburen, Vorden
I./JG300	3		3	Me109 G-14 AS	Altenau, Aschersleben, Hahnenklee,
II./Assault JG300	7	4	11	FW190 A-8	Halberstadt,
III./JG300	7	1	8	Me109 G-14	Nordhausen, Quedlinberg
IV./JG300	1		1	Me109 G-14	
			23		
I./JG301	6	3	9	FW190 A-9/R 11	Brunswick,
II./JG301	3		3	FW190 A-9/R 11	Gottingen
			12		
Total losses (Germany)	37	14	51	(incl 1 *Staffel leader* killed, 1 *Staffel* leader wounded)	

Lack of Training Takes its Toll
November 28th, 1944

Early in the forenoon 1 *Jagddivision* at Döberitz received a report of strong American bomber forces headed towards Berlin. That meant bringing 300 *Jagdgeschwader* to readiness, for its four *Gruppen* had the special role of protecting the capital. But when the bad weather still had not cleared shortly before midday—visibility was down to less than 1 mile in places—the commanding officers considered any attempt at interception out of the question.

Nevertheless two squadrons of 300 *Jagdgeschwader*, I *Gruppe* at Borkheide and II at Löbnitz, were scrambled. Göring, who happened to be at Jüterbog airfield on an inspection that day, pressed *Geschwader* Headquarters and Capt

Nölter's III *Gruppe* to take off. An argument followed between the Commander-in-Chief of the Luftwaffe and Lt Col Dahl, the wing commander, the latter flatly refusing to fly in such weather, since less than half of the 30 pilots briefed for the mission had an instrument-flying qualification. Thus a massed take-off was out of the question and to take off individually would have been suicidal. In the middle of all this elements of 300 *Geschwader's* other two *Gruppe* made contact. But, predictably enough, the moment the pilots broke out of the cloud the American escort flights picked them off, hunted them down and sent them to the ground.

In any event the Americans were not in fact going for Berlin; their target was the fuel industry in Central Germany. More than 1,000 four-engined machines dropped a total of 1,920 tons of bombs, mainly blind, on the installations at Böhlen, Leuna, Lützkendorf and Zeitz.

Reports of German pilots baling out poured into the ops. rooms. About midday the results of the operation became clear; it was ill-conceived and had therefore failed. Only a fraction of the machines that had taken off were still intact. Countless forced landings and parachute descents were recorded. Many had never caught so much as a glimpse of the Americans. The only good thing was that almost all the pilots were able to report back to their units fit for flying.

On the very next day Colonel Lützow, commander of 4 (Training) *Jagddivision* at Altenburg, pronounced on this unsuccessful operation, and in particular on the delay in scrambling III *Gruppe*, 300 *Jagdgeschwader*, and proposed that *every* pilot without exception must be instrument-trained. This requirement was by no means a new one, but no one seemed to have attached much importance to it. This despite the fact that 300 and 301 *Jagdgeschwadern* were designated as 'all weather formations'—the only two of their kind in the whole of the home air defence!

Review of November 1944

Analysis of the Allied offensive air operations of November 1944 shows that, in addition to raids on communications targets, the level of attacks on synthetic fuel production was greatly stepped up. In October the Americans had dropped 12.5% of their total weight of bombs on fuel targets and the RAF 5.9%; but in November these figures rose to 33% and 25% respectively. On the other hand the intensity of strategic operations fell off somewhat from that of the preceding months, as the Americans' attention was focussed on the ground operations that were taking shape in Lorraine and across Belgium and Luxemburg.

On our own side, by contrast, thanks to conservation and accumulation of fighter resources in the previous weeks, we could put strong forces into the air. But the figures are deceptive. The 'Big Punch' envisaged by General Galland, Director of Fighters, never took place. For one thing the weather that November was not suitable for an operation of this kind; the bulk of the pilots lacked the requisite operational training; and in addition the results of operations were falling way below expectations. In the area of I *Jagdkorps* under Lieut-General Schmid, 155 enemy aircraft were shot down for the loss of 404 of our own aircraft, while personnel casualties amounted to at least 300 on the four principal days alone. The November 1944 figure for day-fighter pilots killed or missing, excluding accidents, was 244.

Lt Col Dahl, commander 300 *Jagdgeschwader*, put the situation of the past weeks in a nutshell when he said: 'November 1944's flying was the toughest I had been through in the whole war. The odds were 20 to 1 and often as much as 30 to 1 against us. We were taking casualties every day. Our aircrew reinforcements were short on quality and they didn't get a long enough training. And shortage of fuel was making itself more and more felt.'

Shortage of fuel was indeed becoming more serious and was having its effect on the night fighters too; it was one of the handicaps from which our defence suffered that November, despite isolated successes. A new *Gruppe*, II *Gruppe*, 11 Night-Fighter *Geschwader*, was set up with the specific aim of countering the Mosquito; for these very manoeuvrable British harassing bombers with their high ceiling remained a problem to which the Luftwaffe could offer no real solution. The new squadron was at first equipped with Me109 G-14s, specially modified for night fighting and fitted with the Daimler-Benz 605 AS engine; but these were not man enough for the job. During November the RAF carried out 13 mass night attacks, their main targets being Düsseldorf, Coblenz, Dortmund and various hydrogenation plants in the Ruhr. In the heaviest of these raids, on Düsseldorf, on the night of November 3rd, II *Gruppe*, 1 Night-Fighter *Geschwader*, shot down 10 enemy aircraft in the Höxter area for the loss of only one machine. The overall figures for November 1944 for home air defence night-fighters were 115 kills for 45 aircraft lost.

It is beyond dispute that the general level of activity in this month of November 1944 and the day-by-day response of our fighter pilots evidenced a fighting spirit that words cannot describe. They gave their all in face of an enemy many times stronger—and not altogether without success. Nonetheless it was now plain for all to see that the German fighter force had set its foot on the sacrificial path.

II *The Western Theatre*

Drama Over the Ardennes and the Eifel

Even November's heavy losses did not altogether put paid to the hope, given good weather, of achieving a major success with a mass fighter operation. But by this time Supreme Headquarters had quite a different idea, and preparations were already under way for large-scale operations by all fighter units in support of the planned December offensive in the West. In view of the scope of the ground support operations planned for the fighter force, the first half of the month was taken up by another breathing space to allow at least some units to be brought up to strength with reinforcement aircrew. New aircraft made their appearance too, but the best and most powerful of engines was little use when there was no fuel for it.

Nevertheless, on Major-General Grabmann's figures, December 16th, the day on which the Ardennes offensive opened, saw between 1,600 and 1,800 fighters at readiness. On December 1st the unit strength of aircraft in day-fighter units in I *Jagdkorps* area amounted to rather over 1,000.* But all these figures are misleading; strengths alone do not give a true indication of actual fighting capability. For the pilots of these aircraft, almost to a man, were new and green; their state of training was inadequate, and they were scarcely up to the extreme physical and psychological demands imposed by air combat.

Despite generally unfavourable weather conditions, the strategic air forces in England were very active at the beginning of the month. As early as December 2nd they launched two major attacks on Cologne and Bingen, while US 15th Air Force, based in Italy, bombed the hydrogenation plants and refineries at Blechhammer in Lower Silesia and Floridsdorf near Vienna. The following day the German squadrons were mainly engaged in tactical air support in the Aachen-Düren area and on his side too the enemy committed mainly fighters over Germany. Then on December 4th the Americans put in a large-scale raid on the rail network Kassel-Bebra-Giessen-Mainz.

During this period air defence operations cost the Germans some 65 pilots, 47 of them killed or missing. On December 2nd 3(Udet) *Jagdeschwader* had 19 killed and 5 wounded. Capt Wirges, commanding I *Gruppe*, 3 *Geschwader*, was killed over Damm, near Marburg. Just 24 hours later another squadron commander failed to return. Capt Wienhusen, IV *Gruppe*, 4 *Geschwader*, together with his 14 *Staffel* leader, 1st Lieut Scheufele, were shot down by AA fire on the

* Of which some 650 were serviceable. (Author)

Aachen sector. Scheufele was taken prisoner by the Americans, marking the point at which home air defence had to reckon with the loss of pilots shot down behind the enemy lines and captured as well as of those killed, wounded and missing.

Raids carried out since the beginning of December by the Americans, and to some extent by the RAF, whose heavy bombers were now frequently operating over Germany by day as well as by night, once more made it clear that the enemy was by this time in a position to carry through his attacks regardless of weather conditions in the target area. On December 5th, General Doolittle was ordered to bomb Berlin with his 8th Air Force. The skies above Berlin were completely overcast that day, with 9/10 cloud cover down to 500–1,000ft in places. The forecast was heavy showers with the possibility of storms.

But heaped cumulus and indifferent visibility did not stop the enemy from flying in early that morning over the German capital from the Hanover-Brunswick area with 427 Flying Fortresses. And this date carries another significance too—December 5th, 1944 was the black day of 1 *Jagdgeschwader*.

Despite the November losses and the increasing disruption caused by fuel shortages, 1 *Jagdgeschwader* was able to put some 300 machines into the air, of which, thanks once again to bad weather, the majority failed to intercept. An unusually turbulent wind, gusting up to Force 6 and beyond, was sweeping across wide areas of Central and North Germany, creating an additional problem for pilots on both sides.

Luftflotte Headquarters Germany had earmarked 1 and 301 *Jagdgeschwader* for defence against the force attacking Berlin, and was then forced to commit the battered 27 *Jagdgeschwader*, with IV *Gruppe*, 54 *Geschwader*, under command, against an intrusion by British heavy bombers. The RAF's target was the railway yards at Soest, and this was one of eleven daylight raids made by the RAF during December 1944. With the exception of III *Gruppe*, of which 1st Lieut Clade was acting commander at the time, all 27 *Geschwader's* units took part in the operation. Taking off from the group of airfields Rheine-Achmer-Hopsten-Hesepe, they met the enemy right over the Ruhr. But the British bombers too were well screened by escort fighters. Three Me109s were lost over Gladbeck. One of these lost, Sgt Hornberger, was in fact flying the squadron commander's machine that day, and the double chevrons on the fuselage may have proved fatal by giving the enemy to think that a particularly worthwhile target was being offered them. As to why they had swapped aircraft, only two explanations are likely. On the one hand a changeover of this kind was often made deliberately in some German fighter units to mislead the enemy; on the other this machine may have been fully serviceable while the other had tyre or engine defects or such. Thus the sergeant would switch to the captain's aircraft, because the latter, perhaps, was not flying in this operation or was himself flying some other aircraft, leaving his own available should it be needed.

Over the capital, it was about 1045 when the bomb bay doors opened and their lethal contents tumbled downwards through the unbroken cloud. Up to this moment the American crews had hardly so much as seen a German fighter. On this day too the Mustang escort proved so formidable as to make penetration to the bombers next to impossible. Elements of all three squadrons of 301 *Jagd-geschwader* had been flying on an eastern heading almost parallel to the stream of bombers, apparently without having so far been spotted by the enemy fighter escort.

The men in the Focke-Wulfs had a while to wait before the *Jagddivision* operations centre at Döberitz gave the order to engage. This seemingly endless waiting put an enormous strain on the nerves and was affecting the many inexperienced pilots most of all. Of the enemy nothing was to be seen. Every now and then fighter control passed the latest position of the bomber formation, at the same time correcting its own units' course.

Meanwhile the bombing of Berlin had gone unhindered, and the Americans had turned northeast, headed for Schorf Heath. The whole of 1 (Oesau) *Jagd-geschwader* was now scrambled from Greifwald, Tutow and Anklam to close on the stream of Fortresses and engage it on its way back to England. Then the long-awaited order to go in reached 301 *Geschwader* too. Both *Geschwadern* made contact with the American fighter escort north of the capital somewhere between Oranienburg and Lake Werbellin. The Mustangs immediately went over to the attack in an effort to seal off the bombers completely. But this time they were not flying as far ahead of the bombers as usual, and now and then it was even possible to get a burst off at the real target, the bombers, while taking evasive action against the enemy fighter formations.

It was about midday, over the Uckermark and in particular over the Mecklenburg lakes, that December's first major air battle developed.

II *Gruppe*, 301 *Geschwader*, attacked down the line of the Havel-Oder Canal. But the Mustangs were too much for them; they were forced right off into the Prenzlau-Angermünde area and almost wiped out. I *Gruppe* had thrust further north but also suffered heavy casualties 301 *Jagdgeschwader's* total losses on December 5th amounted to 21 pilots, 18 killed (including II *Gruppe's* commander) and 3 wounded.

The events of the previous month had already made clear how tragic it was that the German fighter force had to be brought up to strength mainly by green reinforcement pilots. This was proved yet again on December 5th, especially in the case of 1 *Jagdgeschwader* which was still undergoing refresher training.

Over Schorf Heath the 8th Air Force bombers turned northwest, presumably on to their final homeward path between Neuruppin and Neustrelitz /Neubrandenburg. Their very strong fighter escort had concentrated on their northern flank; when 301 *Jagdgeschwader* had to break off the engagement, mainly from lack of fuel, the escort turned on 1 *Jagdgeschwader* and the curtain went up on one of the most unfortunate operations in that unit's history.

I *Gruppe* was guided by ground control into map-squares 'Charlie-Foxtrot', 'Charlie-Golf', 'Delta-Foxtrot' and 'Delta-Golf.' No sooner had they reached this area than the Mustang formations spread out like a fan to take the Germans in a pincer movement.

On the western edge of Schorf Heath part of III *Gruppe* was trying to get to grips with the P-51s, while other elements from this *Gruppe* were involved in dogfights further to the north, near Neustrelitz. But II *Gruppe*, 1 *Jagdgeschwader* took a far more punishing blow, with no fewer than 15 pilots killed or missing and 2 wounded. This tragic record made it seem all the more that fate had for once played a kindly trick when Lieut Weissbrodt of 8 *Staffel* who had been seen to crash after a dogfight and whose name already stood on the casualty list, reappeared safe and sound at Tutow. All flights of this Squadron were involved in the Waren area and over Lake Müritz to the south. No one knows how many German fighter pilots were lost on December 5th in this lake, over 40 square miles in area.

Fighter losses on December 5th, 1944

Units taking part	Killed/Missing	Wounded	Total pers/cas	Aircraft	Locality
I/.JG1	6	10	16	FW190 A-8	Furstenberg,
II./JG1	15	2	17	FW190 A-8	Neuruppin,
III./JG1	4	2	6	Me109 G-10/G-14	Neustrelitz,
			39		Rheinsberg, Waren
II./JG2		1	1	FW190 A-8	Bonn
I./JG3	2		2	Me109 G-10/G-14	Steinhuder Meer
IV./JG4	1	2	3	Me109 G-14	Darmstadt, Gosenheim
I./JG26	1		1	FW190 A-8	Furstenau
II./JG27	3	1	4	Me109 G-10/G-14	Dorsten,
IV./JG27	2	1	3	Me109 G-10	Gelsenkirchen, Gladbeck
			7		
IV./JG54	1		1	FW190 A-8	Dortmund
I./JG301	4	1	5	FW190 A-8/R 11	Angermunde, Finow,
II./JG301	7		7	FW190 A-9/R 11	Neustrelitz,
III./JG301	7	2	9	FW190 A-8/R 2	Prenzlau, Schorfheide
			21		
Total losses (Germany)	53	22	75	(incl 1 *Gruppe* commander and 2 *Staffel* leaders killed, 1 *Staffel* leader wounded)	

Gradually the pilots on both sides were forced to break off the engagement. The Americans still had a long flight home ahead of them, and on the German side the red fuel-warning lights were beginning to flicker. But the heavy bombers were still in German airspace and were now in II *Jagdkorps* area. That morning I *Gruppe*, 26 (Schlageter) *Geschwader* based at Fürstenau, had been flying ground support missions over the American penetration in the

Düren-Jülich-Linnich area, where they had already been involved with some Thunderbolts. As all 29 Focke-Wulfs came in to land the squadron commander, Major Borris, found the Inspector of Day Fighters waiting for him. A short extract from I *Gruppe*, 26 *Geschwader*, War Diary tells the rest of the story:

'Landed in at 1041. Major Borris awarded Knight's Cross. Colonel Trautloft orders operations against bombers as they return. Five FW190s airborne at 1315. One Boeing shot down in flames by Borris at 1325; 5 men baled out. Landed at 1345. Nine FW190s airborne at 1432–35. 15.05–15.15—engaged about 50 Thunderbolts without loss. Landed at 1601.'

Luckily the *Gruppe* itself lost only one pilot that day—SWO Buschegger, who crashed on landing at Fürstenau after an engagement with American escort fighters and was killed.

But even before the enemy bombers were back at their bases in England, it had become clear to the staffs at the *Jagddivision* operations centres that the German fighter force had suffered another defeat that day. Against a loss of 75 aircraft only five American bombers were shot down. 8th Air Force reported that 90 German fighters had been destroyed.

The Night Fighters Falter
War Diary Extracts
'12.12.44. Two bomber formations 8th Air Force on Leuna fuel installations and rail targets in Rhine-Main area (Hanau and Darmstadt). Only isolated defensive operations, by 4 and 27 *Jagdgeschwadern*. Major Walter Spies, commander II *Gruppe*, 27 *Geschwader*, killed in action north of Greven. IV *Gruppe*, 4 *Geschwader*—three killed.

I *Gruppe*, 3 *Jagdgeschwader*—mission over the Ruhr against a British four-engined bomber force attacking Witten. Four pilots killed in action.

Ground-support mission in 5 *Jagddivision* area. 53 *Geschwader* reports two pilots killed and one wounded (Sgt Betsch, parachute descent over Dammheim/Landau). Particularly tragic is the loss of WO Scholle, whose parachute failed when he attempted to bale out of his 'White 5'; and of SWO Alexander Preinfalk. Preinfalk, holder of the Knight's Cross, only just 25 and with 78 kills to his credit, was shot by a P-47 while parachuting south-east of Graben (near Bruchsal).'

As already explained, the increasing difficulty of building up the operational picture and, no less important, the need for major fuel savings combined to produce an appreciable impairment of the success of night-fighter operations too. The British had better means at their disposal for deceiving the German early warning system and causing confusion in the fighter control centres, to the point where coordinated large-scale defensive operations by night-fighters became impossible or at least bore little fruit—and this although German night-fighter strength in December 1944 was greater than it had ever been.

The best example of this is the RAF raid on Essen in the evening of December 12th. This once again demonstrated the helplessness of our defence in face of British interference with our radar. That night selected bombers carried, specifically for this purpose, whole batteries of Mandrel sets; when these were switched on a veritable veil was drawn across the German radar systems and identification of the actual bombers beams completely impossible. The Mandrel screen simulated a whole number of radar targets, depriving the German side of any clear idea of the actual course of the enemy operation.

The enemy flew in over the Dutch coast with 633 Lancasters and Halifaxes and was picked up by radar southwest of Aachen just before 1830, heading southeast. I *Jagdkorps* scrambled its night-fighter units and directed them on to Frankfurt/Main, while the British target was in fact Essen. Ten minutes later more night-fighters took off from München-Gladbach. Then at 1906 the radars spotted another enemy formation, and the observer posts had no idea that this was a small group of Mosquitos, which had separated from the main force to make a diversion raid on Osnabrück. A little later, when the target marker flares appeared over Osnabrück, it was assumed that a mass raid was about to take place there. And so at 1927, just three minutes before the actual mass raid on Essen, the night fighters were redirected to the Osnabrück area.

It is true that the main force of heavy bombers emerged clearly from the Mandrel screen just before the attack, but this was taken for a deception raid. At 1937 the night fighters were at last told that Essen was in fact the main target. But confusion became complete when only a short time later they were again given Osnabrück and then, after a few further minutes, told yet once more that Essen was the main target after all. By 1945 RAF Bomber Command's attack was over; the German night fighters were too late.

During December 1944, in the course of 15 major raids, I *Jagdkorps* night fighters achieved 40 kills for a loss of 66 of their own machines. On this basis the overall night-fighter figures for the month amounted to 66 kills and our own losses to 114 machines.

The Ardennes Offensive Begins
Saturday December 16th, 1944
From the early hours of the morning the offensive in the West, the *Wehrmacht's* last great counterstroke, rolled forward. Between Monschau and Echternach, Army Group B under Field Marshal von Rundstedt moved out from its assembly areas to pierce the American line and swept on westwards. The enemy was completely taken by surprise. The offensive had been deliberately timed to coincide with a spell of bad weather; as a result it was only a full week later, on December 23rd, that the Allies were able to make extensive use of their air forces to bring relief to their hard-pressed toops and, still more important, to halt the German advance.

By December 16th too the redeployment of fighter units to the Western front was virtually complete. In effect only two units, 300 and 301 *Jagdgeschwadern* were left to protect Germany itself. And up to that date scarcely a single commanding officer had imagined that Supreme Headquarters would place this quite different interpretation on a 'mass fighter operation.' No longer was the destruction of the enemy in the air, and of his bombers in particular, the main task of home air defence; now they were to be dispersed in low-level strikes on ground targets, in the setting of an offensive which from the very beginning had been built on sand.

For the duration of the offensive all fighter units were placed under command of *HQ Luftflotte* West, which had its operations centre at Limburg. In all there were 12 fighter *Geschwadern* with 40 *Gruppen*, plus two *Gruppen* of 54 *Geschwader* which were under command of other *Geschwader*.

1 *Jagdgeschwader*	3 *Gruppen*
2 *Jagdgeschwader*	3 *Gruppen*
3 *Jagdgeschwader*	4 *Gruppen*
4 *Jagdgeschwader*	4 *Gruppen*
6 *Jagdgeschwader*	3 *Gruppen*
11 *Jagdgeschwader*	3 *Gruppen*
26 *Jagdgeschwader*	3 *Gruppen* (xx + III Gruppe, 54 Wing)
27 *Jagdgeschwader*	4 *Gruppen* (+ IV *Gruppe* 54 *Geschwader)*
53 *Jagdgeschwader*	3 *Gruppen*
77 *Jagdgeschwader*	3 *Gruppen*
300 *Jagdgeschwader*	4 *Gruppen*
301 *Jagdgeschwader*	3 *Gruppen*

With this change of role the *Luftwaffe* High Command had planned for General Peltz, the Director of Bombers (*sic*), to assume command of all fighter units—one more decision that gave rise to great bitterness among fighter commanders at all levels, who saw it not least as another blow for General Galland, the Director of Fighters, whose position had become difficult almost to the point where he had been placed in cold storage. As the coming weeks were to show, it was also a decision which was to have grave consequences.

Over and above this, operational coordination was extremely difficult, for the fighter *Geschwadern* were based much too far from one another—over a breadth of some 250 miles between Oldenburg and the Rhine-Main area.

When the *Wehrmacht* went over to the offensive in the Eifel on December 16th, things were at first very quiet on the German operational airfields. With few exceptions, bad weather kept the units on the ground.

Sunday December 17th, 1944

The second day of the offensive saw little change in the weather; the temperature was 45°F and it rained continuously. But despite the overcast sky, visibility was good enough to allow both sides' fighters to enter the battle. It was remarkable how, in concentrating mainly on logistic targets in the rear areas, the Americans were able to keep the German fighters away from the real scene of the fighting. The air battle in fact took place mainly over the Eifel.

December 17th was the Thunderbolts' and Lightnings' day. Germany, Britain and Russia alike all had good fighter-bombers and close-support aircraft; but perhaps no other type has ever seemed as well cut out for the fighter-bomber role as the Republic P-47 D Thunderbolt. It was its performance that made this aircraft outstanding. Although the heaviest single-engined aircraft used in the Second World War, the Thunderbolt had a top speed of some 375knots at about 30,000ft and excellent dive characteristics. By the same token, it was not just its climb-rate that made the name of the Lockheed P-38

Lightning, which, like the Thunderbolt, was used by the Americans in all theatres. It never ceased to impress German pilots how this twin-fuselaged machine, with its two powerful Allison engines, would be cruising along quietly and then suddenly, without any 'run-up', rocket upwards at overwhelming speed—a manoeuvre which proved fatal for many an unsuspecting German fighter pilot.

It was still morning when things began to hot up to the west of the Rhine. 404th Fighter Group of 9th US TAF was targeted on Bonn-Hangelar airfield, where, as well as a close-reconnaissance unit, 20 Independent Night Close Support *Gruppe* and elements of 55 *Kamptgeschwader* were based. About 0930, 26 FW190s of 26 *Jagdgeschwader* were scrambled in bad weather; they could not find the enemy and returned to Fürstenau without having made contact.

In the meantime however, over Euskirchen, II, III and IV *Gruppe* of 27 *Jagdgeschwader* intercepted the Thunderbolts, which had taken off from St Trond in Belgium. Germans and Americans alike shed their jettison-tanks, and a dogfight rapidly developed. 27 *Geschwader Gruppen* marked up a large number of kills but themselves had 6 pilots killed and 4 wounded. 8 *Staffel* alone lost 4 pilots, including their flight leader, Capt Herbert Rehfeld, killed in action to the east of Aachen.

Thanks to this interception the Hangelar airfield itself remained untouched, so the Americans came back in the afternoon. This time Lt Col Moon sent all three squadrons of his 404 Fighter Group, and once again there was a sharp encounter between the Thunderbolts and the German fighters.

Rheine airfield was harbouring the Me262s of 51 *Kampfgeschwader* in addition to a whole variety of fighter units. Because of this the Allies kept it under constant surveillance, for with their superior performance the jets were at their most vulnerable when taking off and landing. On the morning of December 17th, 5 Hawker Tempests of 56 Squadron, RAF, took off to 'relieve the guard'; south of Nijmegen they met several Me109s from I *Gruppe*, 27 *Jagdgeschwader*. The dogfight which ensued was later joined by more British fighters and ended with the loss of 4 German pilots. The British by contrast landed back at Volkel without loss.

Col Wasem's 474th Fighter Group was operating over the Moselle, in the Trier area. His Lightnings had already been in action that morning, scoring 7 kills without loss; now they reported a further 4 FW190s shot down and 4 others damaged. In this second encounter 474th Group lost 2 machines, and a third P-38 belly-landed near Luxembourg. These may have been the 3 Lightnings shot down by 26 *Jagdgeschwader* on their second sorties of the day Sgt Delor claimed two Lightning kills and Lieut Günther a further one.

26 *Jagdgeschwader* survived the day without loss, but 2 (Richthofen) *Jagdgeschwader* alone reported a further 4 pilots missing, all from its I *Gruppe*.

3, 4 and 11 *Jagdgeschwader* were also involved in the operations of December 17th and took heavy casualties, in particular 4 *Geschwader* with 10 killed, 1 missing and 3 wounded. Michalski, commander 4 *Geschwader*, and his four *Gruppen* were on their way to the Western combat zone. At this time the fighting centred round St Vith, which the Germans had retaken after bitter fighting. But very few machines reached the Belgian-German frontier, for be-

Fighter losses of December 17th, 1944

Units taking part	Killed/ Missing	Wounded	Total pers/cas	Aircraft	Locality
I./JG2	4	1	5	FW190 A-8	Bitburg, Giessen,
II./JG2	4	2	6	Me109 G-6/G-14	Coblenz, St. Vith
			11		
III./JG3	1	2	3	Me109 G-14	Andernach, Bonn
IV./JG3	1	1	2	FW190 A-8	Nierendorf
			5		
I./JG4	3	1	4	Me109 G-14	Birresborn,
II./JG4	3	1	4	FW190 A-8	Boppard, Cochem,
III./JG4	3		3	Me109 G-14/K-4	Heidweiler,
IV./JG4	1	1	2	Me1h9 G-10/G-14	Pronsfeld
			13		
II./JG6	1		1	FW190 A-8	Konigswinter
I./JG11	3	5	8	Me109 G-14	Munstereifel, Wittlich
I./JG27	4		4	Me109 G-14/K-4	Aachen, Beers,
II./JG27	3	3	6	Me109 G-10/G-14	Duren, Eind-hoven
III./JG27	2	1	3	Me109 K-4	Neuenahr
IV./JG27	1		1	Me109 G-10	
			14		
II./JG53		1	1	Me109 G-14	Kandel
IV./JG54	3		3	FW190 A-8/A-9	Bonn, Duren
II./JG300	7	3	10	FW190 A-8	Hochheim, Liegnitz,
III./JG300	2		2	Me109 G-10	Meseritz, Olomouc,
IV./JG300	9	2	11	Me109 G-10/G-14	Prerov, Prossnitz
			23		
Total losses (Germany, Western Theatre and Sudetenland)	55	24	79	(incl 1 *Staffel* leader killed, 1 *Gruppe* commander and 2 *Staffel* leaders wounded)	

Above/Below: Dawn scramble—the start of Operation Baseplate. On the early morning of January 1st, 1945, 33 fighter *Gruppen* were ordered into attacks against the Allied infrastructure in Holland, Belgium and France. The German fighter force's most costly operation was under way. The photographs show two FW 190 A-8s and a D-9 taking off.

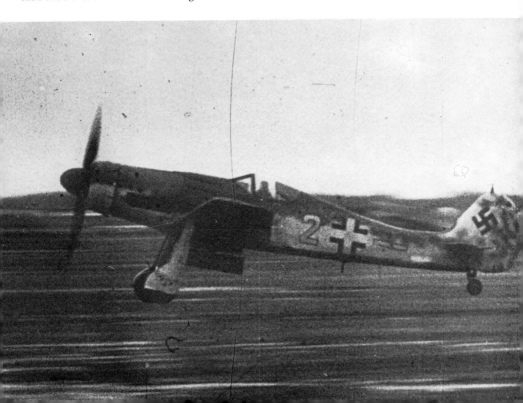

Top: Formation take-off by Messerschmitt Me 109Gs on a snow-covered airfield.

Centre: A fighter *Staffel* flying on an air-defence operation—and (*foot*) in the ground-attack role.

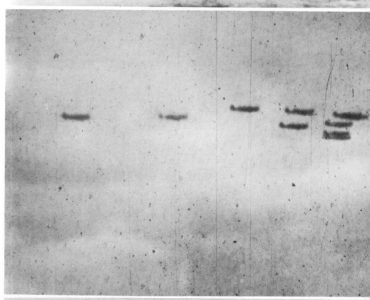

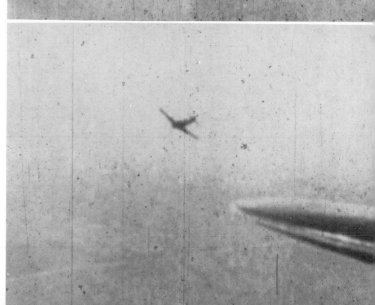

Top: At low level over an enemy airfield. Two Me109s of II *Gruppe*, 11 *Jagdgeschwader* in the surprise attack on Asch airfield in Belgium. But the operation cost 11 *Jagdgeschwader* dear; among the pilots killed or missing was its commander, Lt Col Günter Specht.

Centre: Shot down! A Focke-Wulf is hit and the pilot bales out.

Foot: This photograph, taken somewhere in Belgium or Holland, shows the spot at which a German fighter crashed on January 1st, 1945.

Destroyed on the ground—a burning Lancaster, a Hawker Typhoon and a Spitfire. Operation Baseplate cost the Allied air forces some 400 aircraft, but the enemy was in a position to make these losses good very rapidly. The German fighters' greatest success was at Eindhoven airfield, where the Typhoons of a complete Canadian fighter squadron were destroyed.

Top/Centre: His aircraft riddled with bullets, *Gefreiter* Wagner of 5 *Staffel*, 4 *Jagdgeschwader*, landed on the enemy airfield at St Trond and was taken prisoner by the Americans. His 'White 11', repainted of course, was put to good use by US 404th Fighter Group as a liaison aircraft.

Foot: One of the many crashes in enemy territory on January 1st, 1945. In their forward sectors, the Allies counted in all 137 crashed German fighters.

Above/Right: After a hit in the radiator, Lieut Nibel of 10 *Staffel*, 54 *Jagdgeschwader*, had to make a forced landing at Wennel, northwest of Brussels, and was taken prisoner. Some British soldiers showed great interest in his 'Dora 9', especially in its two MG 131 machine guns.

On a roadside somewhere in Belgium, January 1st, 1945. The end of a FW 190 D-9.

Bachhuber ./JG 54	Oblt. Bartels 3./JG 77	Ogfr. Büttner 3./JG 2	Lt. Doppler I/JG 11	Ogfr. Dworak 3./JG 2
. Gattner ./JG 11	Ofw. Giese 10./JG 11	Lt. Holick 5./JG 1	Fw. Jaschek 15./JG 53	Ofw. Jung 5./JG 6
z. Katzer ./JG 2	Fhr. Leese 14./JG 53	Lt. Ratzlaff 12./JG 53	Fhr. Rosenberger 15./JG 53	Uffz. Richter II./JG 4
rstlt. Specht dre JG11	Fw. Tanck II./JG 77	Oblt. Graf. v. Treuberg 12./JG 3	Fhr. Wiethoff 3./JG 11	Major Vowinckel III./JG 11

Missing on January 1st, 1945. These are only 20 of the fighter pilots of the Luftwaffe who were killed or reported missing, presumed dead, in Operation Baseplate. They represent a far greater number of casualties of this ill-fated New Year mission.

Angriff gegen die Flugplätze im belgisch-holländischen Raum

Großer Erfolg unserer Jagdflieger

Die Heftigkeit der Kämpfe im Raum von Bastogne nahm weiter zu — Geländegewinn an der Saar und in Lothringen — Stärkere sowjetische Angriffe im ungarischen Kampfraum abgewiesen

Schicksalswend

Goldenes Eichenlaub mit Schwertern und Brillanten

Cutting from the Berliner Morgenpost of January 3rd, 1945. The headlines still show no change in tune, and there is of course no mention of the loss of over 200 pilots. (The headlines read:)

'Attack on Dutch and Belgian airfields.
A MAJOR SUCCESS FOR OUR FIGHTERS.
Fighting in the Bastogne area becomes more intense—Our forces gain ground on the Saar and in Lorraine—Heavy Russian attacks repulsed on the Hungarian sector.' (TR)

Focke-Wulf FW190
A-Bs—and their
opponents—in the skies
over Germany. (*Centre*)
Thunderbolts of US 9th
Air Force on operations.
(*Foot*) Mustangs of US
8th Air Force pull out
after a low-level attack.

Above left: Lieut-General Josef Schmid, commander 1 *Jagdkorps*, was in charge of the home air defence units. From December 1st, 1944 to the end of the war he commanded Luftwaffe Headquarters West.

Above right: Col Hajo Herrmann, champion of many new ideas, some of them controversial, commanded 30 *Jagddivision* which he had himself set up with single-engined night fighters, and I *Jagddivision* in the Berlin area. It was on his initiative that 'Special Detachment Elbe' was set up; this formation flew its first and last operation on April 7th, 1945, losing over 70 pilots.

Below: Col Walter Dahl became the last Inspector of Day Fighters, taking over when Col Gollob was appointed Director of Fighters. With III *Gruppe*, 3 *Jagdgeschwader* the 'Special-Purpose *Jagdgeschwader*' and 300 *Jagdgeschwader*, Dahl was outstandingly successful in home air defence, and he was probably the fighter pilot with the highest individual tally of Mustangs.

The North American P-51 D Mustang, one of the deadliest, most manoeuvrable and most stubborn opponents German fighters had to face. Thanks to their great numerical superiority, the Allied fighter forces succeeded again and again in screening their bomber formations from the German air defence, inflicting heavy lossess into the bargain. But not even a Mustang is invincible, as the lower photograph shows.

In the last resort three factors decided the outcome of the war: the offensive against the fuel industry (raid on the hydrogenation plant at Hanover- Misburg— (*top*), the smashing of the German communications network (Giessen marshalling yards, December 24th, 1944— *centre*), and the destruction of German aircraft on the ground (*foot*) throughout Germany itself and the Western theatre as a whole.

Top: The raid by 390th Bombardment Group on the *Wehrmacht* Fuel Depot at Derben-Ferchland, January 14th, 1945. On this day the fighters of 300 and 301 *Jagdgeschwader* once more succeeded in shooting down a fair number of enemy aircraft, but themselves lost 55 pilots in the process.

Above: After take-off, a Me109 G-10/R6 skims the airfield only a few feet up.

Above: Lieut Broeckelschen, one of the few survivors of 'Special Detachment Elbe'. All available machines were assembled to form this force. This G-14 still wears the 3-digit tactical sign of a flying school and, as the ace of spades indicates, has also had a spell with 53 *Jagdgeschwader.*

Below: A German aircraft crashed here. Long after the war was over wreckage like this continued to bear witness to the sacrifice of German fighter pilots.

Above: March 12th, 1945 and the Rhine-Main Airfield is ploughed up by American bombs. Who then would have guessed that it would become Europe's third largest airport? The *Frankfurter Krauz* (top right) motorway intersection, under construction at the time.

Below: The remains of the Luftwaffe, as they were to be found at the end of the war on airfields and airstrips all over Germany.

The end comes. In the middle of April American fighters attacked South German airfields and destroyed hundreds of German machines on the ground (*top*). A last cigarette before facing the rigours of the prison camp. A German fighter pilot with his Me109 G-14 on an American-held airfield (*centre*). The night-fighter force too lies shattered, and the unequal struggle is over (*foot*). But the German fighter pilots had fought with every ounce of their strength, and their efforts had taken an appalling toll in blood. Their splendid achievements should never be forgotten.

hind the Hunsrück 4 *Geschwader* pilots met a force of Thunderbolts. Below the Messerschmitts, although scarcely visible, lay the twists and turns of the Moselle, and at this early stage several machines plunged down through the clouds and were seen no more.

The 'winter battle in the West', as the Press called the offensive, caused the loss of 56 aircrew in German fighter units on December 17th. 27 *Jagdgeschwader*, with 9 killed, 4 wounded and 1 captured, had once again taken the hardest knock; but on this occasion the Wing had 16 kills to its credit. 9th US TAF claimed 68 German fighters destroyed and admitted the loss of 16 aircraft—a figure that would tally exactly with 27 *Geschwader* reports.

That same morning 300 *Jagdgeschwader*, held back in Central Germany, also had to pay a heavy price—not indeed on the Western Front, but over Southeast Germany and the Sudetenland, where engagements between German fighters and Liberator formations with a strong escort were spread over a wide area. The Allies clearly had two purposes in stepping up US 15th Air Force operations. The German counter-offensive increased the importance of destroying the synthetic fuel plants in East Germany, Austria and Poland. At the same time these raids tied down the German home air defence fighters, forcing their withdrawal from planned operations in the Western theatre or at least greatly reducing the strength available for these. These were the reasons for the intrusion of US 15th Air Force bombers into Poland to attack the hydrogenation plant at Auschwitz.

The Americans crossed the Gulf of Trieste in several waves, flying northeast over the eastern part of Austria, and penetrated into the area of Moravia. Action between the intruders and II *Gruppe* 300 *Geschwader*, developed between Osomouc and Přerov and later over Upper Silesia.* II *Gruppe*, now in the assault role and equipped with FW190 A-7s and A-8s, lost 7 killed and 3 wounded here. 5 *Staffel* reported two casualties and 6 *Staffel* four.

Over East Sudetenland and the Klodzko Hills 13 and 14 *Staffel* were trying to get their Messerschmitts through to the American bombers, only to take a knockout punch. This squadron had the heaviest casualties of the day—11 pilots in all.

At the end of the day it was thus clear that, despite a readiness to take risks and press home dashing counter-attacks, the German fighter forces were not up to the task of hampering the execution of the American bombing programme. The Americans came away virtually unscathed, but 300 *Jagdgeschwader's* defensive operations had cost it 23 machines and their pilots, bringing the total losses of German fighter pilots on December 17th to around 80.

But the slaughter was only just beginning.

The Allies Respond

On the third day of the German offensive in the West the weather was again bad —but not bad enough to prevent US 8th Air Force flying in over Germany with some 950 bombers. Dropping their bombs blind through unbroken 10/10 cloud cover, the Americans took as their main targets communications nodes in the rail triangle Coblenz-Ehrang (Trier)-Cologne. That morning and on the days that followed it became evident that the Allies had now shifted the weight of their raids on to communications targets behind the combat zone to stop supplies getting through. Their next reaction to the German offensive was to be the ceaseless pounding of airfields on both sides of the Rhine.

Elements of 1 *Jagdgeschwader* were, it appears, sent up against the bomber incursion, for their 9 *Staffel* reported one man wounded following an engagement with four-engined bombers near Bonn.

9th US TAF was active over Belgium and Luxembourg with twin-engined bomber formations, while its Thunderbolts probed deep behind the line of contact on the hunt for such targets as road convoys, locomotives or concentrations of armour. 77 *Jagdgeschwader* stationed round Dortmund, was committed for the first time. II *Gruppe* and Capt Köhler's III *Gruppe* were tasked to observe the movements of armoured spearheads on the line of contact. But they never got that far, for south of Cologne their Messerschmitts were set upon by the enemy. III *Gruppe* lost three machines. Between Aachen and Bonn, II and III *Gruppe*, 2 *Jagdgeschwader*, were faced by the Thunderbolts of 365th and 368th Fighter Groups. Here our losses were, fortunately, light. Only two pilots failed to return.

On December 18th the Spitfires of British 2nd TAF made their appearance alongside the American fighter hordes. 610 Squadron reported an engagement with some 15 Focke-Wulfs. This was broken off without loss on either side owing to bad visibility; but a British flight leader failed to return for unknown reasons, and a further Spitfire was lost on the squadron's second mission of the day. 66 Squadron on the other hand was more successful. They were briefed to fly a 12-strong armed-reconnaissance mission over Cologne and Coblenz. Over the combat zone they met four vics of Messerschmitts, engaged in some tactical mission, and a dogfight developed in the overcast sky. One Me109 went down in flames and 4 others were damaged; the British lost one Spitfire.

Meanwhile all hell was let loose in the skies around Cologne, where 27 *Jagdgeschwader Gruppen* were involved with a strong force of enemy. When the orders from Headquarters *Luftflotte* West to the units of II *Jagdkorps* reached 3 *Jagdgeschwader* all four *Staffeln* of III *Gruppe* got airborne from their bases below the eastern spurs of the Teutoburger Wald. Capt Langer, the commanding officer of this squadron and an experienced commander, was far from happy; it went against the grain to commit his men to an interception under such appalling weather conditions. He saw the many young faces among his pilots every day and, like other day-fighter COs, he knew only too well the price that this type of operation could and frequently did exact—as it always will. He had already had five of his squadron killed on December 2nd, including his 11 *Staffel* leader, Lieut Karl Willeke.

III *Gruppe's* machines flew down towards the Ruhr before setting course for Cologne, where the messages from ground control told them the enemy bombers were to be found. Southwest of Bonn they suddenly came up against the American fighter escort, and when the battle was over they had lost 8 pilots.

The Wehrmacht Communiqué of December 18th had just this to say:

' . . . German Air Force fighter and close support units covering our troop movements shot down 24 enemy aircraft. The fire of our long-range weapons on London, Antwerp and Liège continues at increased intensity . . . '

Fighter losses December 18th, 1944

Units taking part	Killed/Missing	Wounded	Total pers/cas	Aircraft	Locality
I./JG1	1		1	FW190 A-8	Bonn, Malmedy
III./JG1		2	2	Me109 G-10/G-14	
			3		
II./JG2	2		2	Me109 K-4	Aachen, Bonn
III./JG2	1		1	FW190 A-8	
			3		
III./JG3	5	2	7	Me109 G-14/K-4	Bonn, Dortmund Duren
III./JG6		1	1	Me109 G-6	Andernach
II./JG26		1	1	FW190 D-9	Almelo,
III./JG26	1		1	Me109 K-4	Plantlunne
			2		
II./JG27		1	1	Me109 G-10/G-14 ⎫	
III./JG27	5	2	7	Me109 K-4 ⎬ Cologne, Werl	
IV./JG27	1		1	Me109 G-14 ⎭	
			9		
IV./JG54	2	1	3	FW190 A-8	Cologne, Vussem
I./JG77	2		2	Me109 G-14	Lechenich,
III./JG77	1	2	3	Me109 K-4	Weilerswist, Scheuerheck
			5		
Total losses	21	12	33	(incl 1 *Staffel* leader killed)	
(Germany and Western Theatre)					

The Counter Offensive Mounts

From the early hours of the morning, intense activity reigned in the Allied air bases. US 8th Air Force's heavy bomber units were taking off for Germany, and some 400 light and medium bombers from 9th US TAF were targeted on to the combat zone and the Eifel. The RAF's heavy bombers were to attack Cologne. Strong enemy fighter forces streamed out far in front of the Fortress and Liberator formations to screen their northern flank, for experience had shown that it was from this quarter that the main German fighter threat was likely to come. And on the German side too the fighter units were at readiness; both small formations and large tactical groupings were dispatched to meet the massive Allied incursion.

Air activity on this day was on a scale that had not been seen for some time, for the weather had changed for the better almost overnight and the skies had begun to clear. The depression which had been stationary over the combat zone for a week since December 16th, the day on which the German offensive was launched, was now filling. Here and there the sun even broke through. Fighter pilots on both sides, driven to desperation by the drizzle, snow showers, ground mist and low cloud, now felt more sure of themselves.

With a fighter escort over 400 strong, 417 8th Air Force bombers were directed on to rail junctions west of the Rhine to destroy the German lines of communication. For on the ground German pressure was mounting and the Allied armies were in an awkward position; St Vith had fallen and Bastogne was surrounded.

The American bombers' primary targets were the communication systems in the areas of Trier-Ehrang, Jünkerath-Dahlem and Ahrweiler. At about 1015 a large German fighter formation, around 90 Messerschmitts and Focke-Wulfs from 4, 11, 27 and 54 *Jagdgeschwadern* had passed over Cologne and was now over the triangle Brühl-Bonn-Euskirchen. 4 *Geschwader's* three *Gruppen* flew on southwards undisturbed, but the rest of the force suddenly found swarms of Thunderbolts above their heads. These were the battle-proven pilots of Col Schilling's 56th Fighter Group; in a flash they had dropped their jettison tanks and were diving on their enemy. The German pilots realised the danger, but the P-47s, coming from above, had the edge.

Just over Kottenforst a damaged FW190 broke away and tried to get clear of its pursuers, but near Röttgen the pilot, Sgt Willi Bach of 16 *Staffel*, 54 *Geschwader*, crashed to his death still in his machine. At about 1030, a second FW190 A-8 from the same wing appeared over the tree-tops and went down near the hamlet of Villip. This machine too had been hit earlier on, and Sgt Klaus Gehring from Gerdauen in East Prussia had decided to bale out. But he failed to jump clear; his parachute fouled on the tail and he was killed when the aircraft struck. Only a few hundred yards away, near the moated castle of Gudenau, a Messerschmitt struck with an incredibly violent impact and buried itself deep in the frozen ground. No parachute was seen, and it was to be 24 years, almost to the day, before more was known of this crash. It was the Me109 G-10 of SWO Heinrich Bartels, who had destroyed a Thunderbolt just before he was himself shot down. This was the 99th kill scored by this 26-year-old holder of the Knight's Cross from Linz on the Danube, who had been flying with IV *Gruppe* 27 *Jagdgeschwader*, since May 1943.

The three *Gruppen* from 4 *Jagdgeschwader*, together with I *Gruppe* of Lt Col Günther Specht's 11 *Geschwader* tried to carry on with their mission and intercept the American bomber formations before the latter reached Trier. But this intention was largely frustrated by the enemy fighter escort and these units became involved in dogfights which spread out right across the Eifel.

Major Jeffrey of 479th Fighter Group personally accounted for three of the 12 FW190s shot down by his formation, this for the loss of one Mustang. 8 *Staffel*, 4 *Jagdgeschwader* was the heaviest sufferer here.

But 11 *Jagdgeschwader* was in far worse plight. With 12 pilots killed and 4 missing it accounted for the bulk of the German losses on December 23rd. Its three *Gruppen* were scattered over the whole area of operations; I *Gruppen* together with IV *Gruppe*, 4 *Geschwader*, succeeded in taking on the heavy bombers over the Moselle. The other two *Gruppen*, operating under command of 3 (Udet) *Jagdgeschwader*, encountered fighter escorts from both 8th Air Force and 9th US TAF.

Using the fine weather to good effect, 9th US TAF's fighter-bombers gave their ground troops all possible support. C-47 transport wings were at last able to drop food, ammunition and equipment to their troops surrounded at Bastogne, but German AA shot down 8 of these aircraft. Before the morning was over 624 two-engined bombers, A26 Invaders and B26 Marauders, were on their way to take out the rail system immediately behind the line of contact. 9th Bombardment Division suffered its heaviest losses so far; German AA and home air defence fighters shot down 30 bombers; a further 6 crashed or made forced landings later; and over 180 were damaged. Among 9th US TAF's first targets were the yards at Ahrweiler, which were bombed by some 60 Marauders from 386th and 391st Bombardment Groups. But suddenly about an equal number of grey fighters made their appearance—part of the tactical grouping made up from 2, 3 and 11 *Jagdgeschwader*. The Germans concentrated on the second wave of bombers as they flew on towards the Westerwald and accounted for 16 Marauders from the 391st Group.

But our own losses were higher. III *Gruppe*, 2 *Jagdgeschwader* lost five pilots. Two were reported missing; WO Heinz Schneider has never been traced, but in January 1968 the body of Sgt Burger of 12 Flight was found near Meckenheim on Swistbach in his FW190 D-9, one of the first of this 'long-nosed' mark to be lost in the West.

3 *Jagdgeschwader* reported four parachute descents. One of these was Cadet Adolf Tham, who was injured when he rammed a Marauder with the Me109 K-4. The others may have been the crew of one of the two B26s reported lost by 322nd Bombardment Group. This Group was attacking the rail bridges at Euskirchen when it was set upon by 20–30 German aircraft, of which about 6 were lost.

For some 70 Marauders of 387th and 394th Bombardment Groups the target was the railway yards at Mayen. But before they got there several vics of German fighters dived onto them. Here the result was four all, but these fighter units suffered further losses in intercepting a raid by twin-engined bombers on the Moselle bridges between Cochem and Eller, where the Germans scored seven kills for the loss of eight aircraft.

Bomber waves and fighter formations flying to and fro had years since become a daily event in the lives of the population of the area between Aachen and Cologne, but the drama that was enacted on December 23rd over the bleak, snow-covered slopes of the Eifel looked like the first act of a tragedy. Never had these countryfolk seen so many aircraft drop out of the sky.

Meanwhile 12 *Staffel* 11 *Jagdgeschwader* must have encountered the enemy over the High Eifel in the triangle St. Vith-Prüm-Stadtkyll. Somewhere over this wild country, it is presumed, Major Erich Putzka of Headquarters III *Gruppe*, 11 *geschwader* who remains untraced, was shot down in his FW190 A-8; and the same applies to SWO Holland, last seen in a dogfight with around 30 Thunderbolts. SWO Titscher was also killed, having been shot down —according to his fellow pilots—by a Spitfire. This may well have been correct; the RAF carried out a daylight raid on Cologne at about this time on December 23rd and the bombers did have a fighter escort.

Throughout the morning the skies between Aachen and Saarbrücken had been the scene of a ding-dong battle, the most intensive for weeks; but in the afternoon activity died down. The German fighter units were exhausted. Pilots

Fighter losses on December 23rd, 1944

Units taking part	Killed/Missing	Wounded	Total pers/cas	Aircraft	Locality
I./JG1	1	1	2	FW190 A-8	Bocholt,
III./JG1		1	1	Me109 G-14	Dortmund, Wesel
			—		
			3		
I./JG2	2		2	FW190 A-8/D-9	Aachen, Bastogne,
II./JG2	3	1	4	Me109 G-14	Marienberg,
III./JG2	5		5	FW190A-8/D-9	Meckenheim, Siegburg
			—		
			11		
I./JG3	1		1	Me109 G-14	Adenau, Meckenheim,
III./JG3	1	1	2	Me109 G-14/K-4	St. Vith
IV./JG3	2	3	5	FW190 A-8	
			—		
			8		
I./JG4		1	1	Me109G-14	
II./JG4	6		6	FW190 A-8	Nurburg, Roth
III./JC4	3	3	6	Me109 G-10/K-4	St. Vith, Trier
IV./JG4	3		3		
			—		
			16		
I./JG11	6	5	11	FW190 A-8	Adenau, Gillenfeld,
II./JG11	3	3	6	Me109 G-14	Kaisersesch,
III./JG11	7	3	10	FW190 A-8	Coblenz, Mayen, St. Vith
			—		
			27		
I./JG26	4	2	6	FW190 A-8	Duren, Cologne,
II./JG26	1	1	2	FW190 D-9	Nettersheim
			—		
			8		
II./JG27	2		2	Me109 G-10/G-14	Bonn, Rhine-Main,
III./JG27		1	1	Me109 K-4	Villip
IV./JG27	1		1	Me109 G-10	
			—		
			4		
II./JG53	1	2	3	Me109 G-14 AS	Rastatt, Wagshurst,
III./JG53	1		1	Me109 G-14	Weissenburg
			—		
			4		
IV./JG54	2		2	FW190 A-8	Villip, St. Vith, Liege
I./JG77	6	2	8	Me109 G-14	Altenahr,
III./JG77	2	5	7	Me109 K-4	Houverath, Lessenich,
			—		
			15		Neuenahr
Total losses (Germany and Western Theatre)	63	35	98	(incl 1 *Staffel* leader killed)	

who had baled out over the various zones of the action were trying to get back to their units, being taken off to nearby hospitals by the ground troops and the Eifel farmers, or even falling into enemy hands. Bodies were being recovered from shattered machines, and the countryfolk would gaze at the charred, twisted strips of scrap metal and the broken bodies within them and wonder what kind of sense it all made.

But meanwhile 9th US TAF had despatched a fresh force of over 200 twin-engined bombers with a Thunderbolt escort. It was shortly after midday when Capt Köhler received orders for his III *Gruppe* in 77 *Jagdgeschwader*. As the *Gruppe* took off from their base at Düsseldorf-Unterrath at about 1345, the pilots were hardly to know that not a single one of them would reach their destination round Bastogne. Heading south, the Messerschmitt Me109 K-4s first overflew Cologne, intending to turn west over the top of the Ahr Hills and make for the combat zone. And it was just over the Ahr valley that 11 and 12 *Staffel* were surprised by a pack of enemy fighters. 11 *Staffel* under Lieut Hackler escaped with only two pilots wounded; but Lieut Staroste would always remember the day when the Americans carved up his 12 *Staffel*. He had one pilot in three killed or wounded.

Scattered by the enemy pursuit, the German machines came in by dribs and drabs at airfields all over the place, and it was 1515 when the two Me109s of the *Gruppe* commander and his adjutant, 1st Lieut Kleber, touched down at Cologne-Wahn.

53 (Ace of Spades) *Geschwader* lost four pilots in the day's operations. So one of the costliest days since the home air defence forces had been set up drew to its close. Despite involvement in innumerable encounters with a good number of kills to its credit, the fighter force had been unable to hamper the enemy's plan of attack. Thanks to its formidable fighter escort, US 8th Air Force was able to hold its losses to two four-engined bombers and 15 fighters; but 9th US TAF lost 35–40 light and medium bombers, some of them accounted for by AA fire.

Of the 450–500 German fighter pilots who took part in the operations of December 23rd, 1944, records show 63 killed, missing or taken prisoner and 35 wounded. The Allied air forces, on the other hand, claimed 116 German fighters shot down and 11 probables.

No Christmas Truce
Sunday December 24th, 1944

In I and II *Jagdkorps*, preparations to deal with a major Allied incursion went ahead on a scale not seen since the Allied landings. It was little short of a miracle that, less than twenty-four hours after its costly air battles in the West, the fighter force could resume its defensive operations with 700—800 machines at its disposal. It was largely thanks to the 'men in black' of the ground staff that, after repeated sorties the day before, these machines stood ready on the tarmac in the morning. The measure of these men's achievement can be truly appreciated only by those who know how many Messerschmitts and Focke-Wulfs had come in with battle-damage, engine faults or other technical defects, or had even been prevented by hydraulic failures from leaving the ground. Botching those machines up again in the few hours available called for a high sense of responsibility, unsparing effort and immense attention to detail.

The fighter force had good reason to draw itself up in such strength, for the bad weather of the preceding week had now finally cleared, and December 24th dawned with a clear blue sky; cloud cover over Cologne, for instance, was only 1/10. It was not very hard to guess that the enemy would use this weather to put a stop to von Rundstedt's offensive once and for all. US 8th Air Force put 2,034 bombers into the air that morning—the largest single operation in its history. 1,400 bombers, with a 700 strong fighter escort, concentrated their bombs on eleven German airfields in the Giessen, Frankfurt and Darmstadt areas; the rest, supported by RAF and 9th US TAF formations, attacked communications targets, mainly railway installations between Trier and Euskirchen.

As the leading Flying Fortresses appeared over Germany, the last heavy bombers were just clearing the English coast—a veritable armada, under the command of Brigadier-General Frederic Castle. Headed by IV *Gruppe*, the former assault *Gruppe*, 3 *Jagdgeschwader* was one of the first German formations to close the tight-packed enemy bombers. Behind every control column sat a pilot known to be well-versed in air defence; not a few of the rudders were well 'notched'. Once again the men of 13, 14 and 15 *Staffeln* were determined to give the enemy a really warm welcome.

IV Squadron spotted the leading bombers just in front of Liège. The American fighter escort was not yet in position, so the Focke-Wulfs were able to open the engagement with a frontal attack. In a trice four B 17s were plunging earthwards in flames, and five others were so badly hit that they had to make forced landings. But meanwhile the Mustangs had appeared and were trying to force the attackers back. IV *Gruppe*, 3 *Geschwader* became involved in a really vicious dogfight. Capt Wolfgang Kosse, 13 *Staffel* leader, and SWO Egon Schulz broke away from the formation and have still never been traced; and five other pilots, were shot down by the heavy bombers' gunners or the enemy fighter escort, all being taken prisoner. Right across the board, 3 *Jagdgeschwader* had the largest number reported missing that day. However one of the Flying Fortresses shot down was flown by Brig-Gen Castle, one of the ablest commanders in US 8th Air Force. Castle gave his crew the order to bale out, but by then it was too late for him to get clear himself and he dived to his death in the heavy bomber.

Heading east on a slightly zig-zag course the formations pressed on and crossed the German frontier south of Aachen. While 3 *Jagdgeschwader* hung on to the enemy and shot down quite a few more bombers, I *Gruppe*, 27 *Jagdgeschwader* and all three squadrons of 6 *Jagdgeschwader* were sent in; fierce infighting developed over the High Venn. More and more vapour trails sliced across the blue sky, the tragic beauty of their curves, rings, wave-patterns and whorls bearing witness to watchers on the ground of the progress of the fierce battle.

At 13,000 feet it was bitterly cold, and thus another hazard lay in wait for the young pilots—icing. No one knows how many pilots succumbed to icing, but it may well be that some of those reported missing were not in fact killed in action and that their remains lie hidden for ever in the wild heathland and bogs of the

Venn.

To the north of Aachen and over the Ruhr, hordes of Spitfires, Typhoons and Tempests from 2 TAF were on patrol; but the intensity of the German fighter force's operations that day surprised even the British. Their opponents, I and III *Gruppe*, 3 *Jagdgeschwader*, two *Gruppe* of 26 *Jagdgeschwader* from 27 *Geschwader* and IV *Gruppe*, 54 *Geschwader*, had in fact been tasked against the American bomber incursion and now had to abandon their original mission and take on the British. 193 Squadron suddenly spotted over 50 Messerschmitts and Focke-Wulfs in process of shooting down one Hawker Typhoon and damaging another. This was probably IV *Gruppe*, 27 *Geschwader*, and IV *Gruppe*, 54 *Geschwader*. 10 British fighters which were just over West Münsterland and heard the contact over the RT turned to rush to the help of their friend, only to be engaged by German fighters coming at them out of the sun.

Other fighter units reported engagements between Malmédy and Eindhoven. Then, when further contact was made between the Rhine and the Dutch-German border, control of the German defensive operation seemed to be lost. Nobody knew any more where or with whom units were involved.

77 *Jagdgeschwader* had an extremely fraught day's fighting, its I *Gruppe* taking heavy casualties from British and American fighters in an operation against 9th US TAF. In a short space of time the Wing lost a dozen Messerschmitts, with 8 pilots killed and 1 missing.

Across the Rhine, escorting Mustangs and Lightnings suddenly fanned out ahead of the bomber groups to screen the eastern flank of the US 8th Air Force raids on the Rhine-Main area; the Americans must have known they were getting into the operational area of those two well-tried formations, 300 and 301 *Jagdgeschwader*. The bomber force now split into two mass formations; one headed for 4 and 11 *Jagdgeschwader* airfields, while the other turned for 2 *Jagdgeschwader* bases. Elements of I, II and III *Gruppen*, 4 *Jagdgeschwader*, scrambled from their strips along the Frankfurt-Darmstadt autobahn to meet the Flying Fortresses in map-squares 'Papa-Quebec / Quebec-Quebec'—in the Mosell-Rhine triangle south of Coblenz. Almost on first contact two Focke-Wulfs from 5 *Staffel* were shot down and their pilots killed. While bombs and strafing were ploughing up their runways at Biblis, Gross-Ostheim and Zellhausen, almost the whole of 11 *Jagdgeschwader* was involved with the Liberator formations of 2(US) Air Division. Three pilots were killed in action. The second 8th Air Force bomber formation's target was five airfields in the general area of Giessen, mainly occupied by Lt Col Bühligen's 'Richthofen' *Jagdgeschwader*—Ettingshausen, Giessen, Merzhausen, Nidda, and Kirch-Göns. German fighter opposition was slight here; the Americans had already pinned down the bulk of the German fighter force west of the Rhine, or captured. With 21 wounded pilots on top of this, aircrew losses on a single day were at least 106, or probably over 12% of those taking part in the German operations as a whole. The American and British air forces claimed 125 German fighter kills and five probables.

The destruction of 44 four-engined bombers bears witness to the intensity of the fighting and the determination of the German fighter pilots. But in the last resort all this could not hide the fact that the German fighter force could no

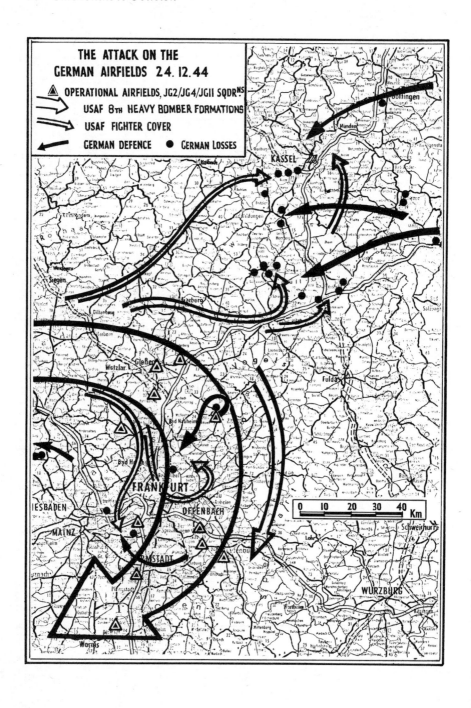

THE ATTACK ON THE
GERMAN AIRFIELDS 24.12.44

△ OPERATIONAL AIRFIELDS, JG2/JG4/JGII SQDRNS

⇨ USAF 8TH HEAVY BOMBER FORMATIONS

⇨ USAF FIGHTER COVER

◂ GERMAN DEFENCE   ● GERMAN LOSSES

Fighter losses on December 24th, 1944

Units taking part	Killed/Missing	Wounded	Total pers/cas	Aircraft	Locality
I./JG1	1	1	2	FW190 A-8	Aachen,
II./JG1	1		1	FW190 A-8	Monchen-gladbach,
III./JG1	2		2	Me109 G-14	St. Vith
			5		
II./JG2	3		3	Me109 G-14	Aachen, Bastogne
I./JG3	6		6	Me109 G-10	Ardennes-Eifel,
III./JG3	4		4	Me109 G-14/K-4	Liege, St. Vith
IV./JG3	7		7	FW190 A-8/A-9	
			17		
I./JG4		1	1	Me109 G-14	Boppara,
II./JG4	2		2	FW190 A-8	Morfelden,
III./JG4	1		1	Me109 G-10	Wiesbaden
			4		
I./JG6	9		9	FW190 A-8/A-9	Aachen, Eupen,
II./JG6	2		2	FW190 A-8	Cologne, Liege
III./JG6	2		2	Me109 G-14	
			13		
I./JG11	2	1	3	FW190 A-8	Alzey, Trier
III./JG11	3	1	4	FW190 A-8	
			7		
I./JG26	4	1	5	FW190 A-8/A-9	Haltern, Liege,
II./JG26	3	1	4	FW190 D-9	Malmedy, Rheine
			9		
I./JG27	4	1	5	Me109 G-14/K-4	Bochum, Bonn,
II./JG27	1	1	2	Me109 G-10	Dyk, Hattingen,
III./JG27		1	1	Me109 K-4	St. Vith
IV./JG27		2	2	Me109 G-10/G-14	
			10		
IV./JG53	1	1	2	Me109 G-14	Neustadt, Rottweil
IV./JG4	3	1	4	FW190 A-8/A-9	Liege, Setterich
I./JG77	9	1	10	Me109 G-14	Antweiler,
III./JG77	1		1	Me109 K-4	Euskirchen, Hoscheid,
			11		Munstereifel
II./JG300	6	7	13	FW190 A-8	Eschwege, Fritzlar
III./JG300	2		2	Me109 G-10	Gottingen,
IV./JG300	3		3	Me109 G-10AS	Hersfeld, Kassel, Ziegenhain
			18		
I./SG4	1		1	FW190 F-8	Bastogne
II./SG4	2		2	FW190 F-8	
			3		
Total losses (Germany and Western Theatre)	85	21	106	(incl 2 *Gruppe* commanders and 5 *Staffel* leaders killed or missing, 1 Geschwader wounded	

longer carry out its mission of hampering enemy operations in the combat zone and over Germany and inflicting significant losses. And the fighter pilots' mistrust of their leadership continued to grow; for a long time now they had had the feeling that they were being sacrificed to no good purpose.

The inevitable encounter with units of 300 and 301 *Jagdgeschwadern* came, as the Americans had foreseen, during the return flight over North Hesse.* The German fighters, flying in from Thuringia, engaged the enemy in several waves, with the result that the extremely bitter fighting was spread out from the Knüll Hills to the Göttingen area. Major Peters, who owing to a leg injury had to command his III(Assault) *Gruppe* (300 *Geschwader*) from the ops room, duly recorded his pilots' kill reports—but also the mounting losses. Lieut Bretschneider, who was leading the squadron's tactical formation that day, was bettered by a Mustang pilot in a sharp encounter over the southern slopes of the Knüll Hills, and went down in his A-8 'Red 1', known as 'Raubatz VII', at Hausen, near Oberaula. Lieut Bretschneider, Knight's Cross, 5 *Staffel* leader, had scored a total of 31 kills, over half of them in single-engined night fighters, in only 20 operational sorties.

The major air battle was drawing to an end. A few hours later, as the darkness closed in on Christmas Eve and, in this fifth Christmas of the War, men could wish for no greater blessing than the coming of peace, nobody knew the terrible price that the day's operations had really cost the German fighter force. The day's losses were never finally established; at *Jagddivision* and in *Luftflotte* Headquarters West the staff had no real picture of the true scale of the defeat.

Only much later did it become clear that December 24th fighter pilot casualties amounted in fact to 85 killed, or missing.

Monday December 25th 1944

Christmas Day, 1944, and the Ardennes offensive was nearing its climax; already the indications were there that the German troops could advance no further and that the Allies were beginning to firm up their defensive positions and even go over to the counter-attack. By their massive operations against communications targets just behind the combat zone, the enemy air forces were succeeding in cutting the German lines of communication to the point where supplies were reaching the front line only with great difficulty if at all.

The German fighter pilots can hardly be held to blame for having only to a very limited extent accomplished their assigned task of tactical support for the advance; on the contrary they showed a magnificent fighting spirit in an unaccustomed role—and it cost them dear. There was scarcely a single fighter unit that was not intercepted on its way to the target by overwhelmingly superior forces of Mustangs, Thunderbolts, Spitfires, Typhoons or Tempests and forced to give battle. Over this Christmas of 1944 the fighter force received its mortal blow; within a bare two weeks it was to be finally wiped out.

During the morning of December 25th, Hawker Typhoons of 193 and 266 Squadrons 2nd TAF took off for low-level attacks in the area north of the Ruhr, while over Duisburg the Spitfires of 401 Squadron lay in wait for their prey.

---

* See map. It appears that the bomber forces turned away southwest while the bulk of the fighter escort swung east and northeast to screen them. (Tr)

Both squadrons soon encountered German home air defence fighters, and dogfights developed. Pieces of a shot-down Me109 struck Squadron Leader Everard's machine, forcing him to bale out.

II *Gruppe*, 26 Fighter Wing, had two casualties that day, 26 *Geschwader* reported only two kills, two fewer than 27 *Jagdgeschwader*, whose four *Gruppen* missions dispersed them over the whole Western operational area. But 27 *Geschwader* took a really punishing blow; with 13 pilots lost it suffered the heaviest casualties of any formation that day.

The Me109 G-14s of I *Gruppe*, 3 *Jagdgeschwader*, flew from their base at Paderborn with the mission of providing air cover for our armoured forces round Liège. But they never got there. About noon they were attacked south of Bonn by Mustangs in strength. Southeast of Düren, 125 Group, RAF, scored its hundredth kill since D-Day when Flight Lieutenant Sherk of 402 Squadron, flying a Spitfire, shot down an isolated FW190. The German pilot, whose parachute failed to open, may have been Sgt Wolfgang Rosenow of 11 *Staffel*, 11 *Jagdgeschwader*, whose FW190 A-8 was reported missing near Euskirchen.

Shortly after midday some pilots of 411 Squadron spotted a lone Me262, apparently going in to land at Rheine airfield. This was '9K+MM' from II *Gruppe*, 51 *Kampfgeschwader* (Fighters), with 1st Lieut Lamle in the seat, on his way back from a sortie over Liège. He spotted the enemy fighters coming up on his tail but had already throttled back and lost too much speed to get away. He was shot down by Flight Lieutenant Boyle at about 1230 and was killed. That same afternoon the British destroyed another Me262. 403 Squadron intercepted a vic of these jet fighters near Eupen, and Squadron Leader Collier shot one down.

The Americans were heading for the German frontier when they were engaged over the High Venn by strong formations from 1 and 3 *Jagdgeschwader*. The whole of IV *Gruppe*, 3 *Geschwader*, under its commander Capt Hubert-York Weydenhammer, was in the air that afternoon. Covered by the Messerschmitts of III *Gruppe* 1 *Jagdgeschwader* the Germans got right in amongst the bomber formations. The first Liberators were soon dropping out of the sky into the woods between Liège and St Vith, and the fighters succeeded in shooting down a whole string of bombers, mainly from the 467th Bombardment Group. But then their turn came, as 479th Fighter Group's Mustangs took them in the rear and split the German tactical formation wide open. Capt Weydenhammer was seen going in to attack a Liberator, but at that point the situation became confused. No trace has ever been found of Capt Weydenhammer, nor of WO Clässen, Sgt Gaspers or S/Cadet Vaitl. According to enemy sources, the American fighter group engaged some 12-15 Focke-Wulfs, which were themselves attacking the Liberator formation. They shot two German fighters down, literally chasing a FW190 right into the ground. Presumably at least one of the missing pilots from IV *Gruppe*, among them the *Gruppe* commander, was killed in these two aircraft. Two of the *Gruppe*' pilots, Lieut Mebesius and Sgt Wagner, came down over Belgium and were taken prisoner by the Americans. WO Hoffmann on the other hand managed to dive clear of the fighters only to

---

* 51 Wing was equipped with the Me262 in the 'hit-and-run' bomber role and later posted to the Rheine area and switched to the fighter role. Hence the mixed designation—KG(J)51. (Tr.)

be caught in Allied flak, and landed back at Cologne-Wahn with his FW190 like a sieve.

Fighter losses on December 25th, 1944

Units taking part	Killed/ Missing	Wounded	Total pers/cas	Aircraft	Locality
II./JG1	1	1	2	FW190 A-8	Hohes, Venn,
III./JG1	7	2	9	Me109 G-10/G-14	Liege, Marche
			11		
I./JG3	2	1	3	Me109 G-14	Liege, St. Vith
III./JG3	1		1	Me109 G-14	
IV./JG3	7		7	FW190 A-8	
			11		
III./JG6	4	1	5	Me109 G-14	Cologne, Quakenbruck
I./JG11	2		2	FW190 A-8	Bitburg, Euskirchen,
III./JG11	4		4	FW190 A-8	Siegburg
			6		
II./JG26	2		2	FW190 D-9	Dortmund, Furstenau,
III./JG26	1		1	Me109 K-4	Horneburg
			3		
I./JG27	1	2	3	Me109 G-10/G-14	Aachen, Adenau,
II./JG27	2	4	6	Me109 G-10/G-14	Malmedy, Mayen
III./JG27	1		1	Me109 K-4	Neuenahr,
IV./JG27	2	1	3	Me109 G-10/G-14	Nurburgring
			13		
II./JG53	2		2	Me109 G-14	Hochspeyer,
III./JG53	1		1	Me109 G-14	Oberharmersbach
			3		
IV./JG54	8		8	FW190 A-8/A-9	Jammelshofeh, Kempenich
I./JG77	1	1	2	Me109 G-14	Ollheim
Total losses (Germany and Western Theatre	49	13	62	(incl 1 *Gruppe* commander and 1 *Staffel* leader killed, or missing, 1 *Gruppe* commander wounded)	

1 *Jagdgeschwader* with 11 casualties, could scarcely be said to have come through this mission unscathed. Major Preddy, commanding 352nd Mustang Group, one of the American fighter aces, scored his 26th and 27th kills that

day. But he himself did not return to base; he was hit by his own side's flak while crossing the line of contact and was killed when he crashed near Liège. The same thing happened to Lieut Bouchier of 479th Fighter Group but he landed safely by parachute.

Numerous small groups of twin-engined bombers from 9th US TAF—629 sorties in all—put in further attacks on the road and rail network behind the line of contact, concentrating on the area between Cologne and Coblenz. Against them *Luftflotte* Headquarters West sent in III *Gruppe*, 6 *Jagdgeschwader*, I and III *Gruppen*, 11 *Geschwader*, 27 *Geschwader* complete, IV *Gruppe*, 54 *Geschwader* and I *Gruppe*, 77 *Geschwader*. The fact that they frequently met British fighters instead of the Americans they expected, or vice versa, serves to characterise the scale and scope of Allied air operations over Western Germany at that time.

On the following day the supreme Headquarters communiqué read: 'Yesterday German fighter units again intercepted strong enemy formations and prevented them from bombing their intended targets.' What the man in the street was not told was that on 25th December the German fighter force once again lost over 60 aircraft with more than 40 pilots killed.

War Diary Extract

'*26.12.44*. Very cold. The Americans and British appeared only in limited strength, and the intensity of our own operations was diminished.

II *Gruppe* 1 *Jagdgeschwader* had the day's heaviest losses. Eight pilots failed to return and were reported missing. The Squadron was involved in dogfights round Bastogne.

Fifteen 'long-noses' from I *Gruppe*, 26 *Jagdgeschwader* led by 1st Lieut Hartigs, were airborne at 1058 and became involved with Mustangs over Belgium. 1st Lieut Hartigs (4 *Staffel*.) and Sgt Schöndorf (1 *Staffel*.) were taken prisoner near Carlsbourg. SWO Schwarz reported a kill, but AC Bergmeier and Sgts Grad and Sattler were killed in action.

27 *Jagdgeschwader* also had 6 pilots killed in the Liège area.

In the southwest, II *Gruppe*, 53 *Jagdgeschwader*, had contact with an American incursion in the Stuttgart area. Capt Meimberg, the *Gruppe* leader, was shot down and baled out over Schaichhof. 1st Lieut Ludolf met a tragic end at Rutesheim; he jumped when too low, and the parachute did not have time to deploy fully. *Gefreiter* Ruland (8 *Staffel*) was wounded and made a belly-landing near Flacht. *Gefreiten* Meermann (6 *Staffel*) was shot down and killed east of Wimsheim.

4 Close Support *Geschwader* (FW190 F-8s) lost four pilots, including two *Staffel* leaders. Capt Jungelausen (3 *Staffel*) and Capt Schürmer (1 *Staffel*) were killed in action in map square 'Lima-Kilo' north of the Soon Woods. SWOs Weinreich and Zumkeller were reported missing.'

The Ardennes Offensive is Halted

After twelve days of winter warfare the Western Allies succeeded in breaking out of the encircled and bitterly contested town of Bastogne and in bringing the German offensive to a halt once and for all. The German troops had reached the limit of their penetration. Their spearheads were in front of Dinant, within sight of the Meuse; but they lacked the strength to push farther ahead, and their losses were many times greater than had been expected.

The cold, clear winter weather held, and yet again the enemy's superior forces dominated the airspace over the combat zone. In addition over 1,000 heavy bombers from US 8th Air Force flew into the Rhineland to bomb communications targets in the Coblenz area; and once more the swarms of Mustangs fanned out far ahead of the bombers to screen their northern flank.

Capt Ehlers led his I *Gruppe*, 1 *Jagdgeschwader*, on a tactical support mission in the Dinant area. But just west of Mayen, in the Eifel, they became involved in a large-scale air battle and lost nine pilots. At the head of the list stood Capt Hans Ehlers' name; he crashed in his Focke-Wulf 'White 20' near Bereborn, at the foot of the 2,200 ft Hochkels.

II *Gruppe*, 2 *Jagdgeschwader*, took part in the same operation but escaped with two wounded. St Trefzer baled out at Wershofen, north of Antweiler, after a dogfight with some 20 Mustangs; and Cadet-WO Alfred Richter put his Me109 G-14 down in a forced landing about 20 miles away, near Brühl.

27 *Jagdgeschwader* was again tasked to provide air cover over the leading infantry, and this time most of them managed to get through to the Bastogne area. Lieut Beckmann, whose 4 *Staffel* was flying top cover, suddenly spotted two P-38 Lightnings and shot one down. As the American fighter disappeared from view southeast of Bastogne, the *Staffel* met a bunch of Mustangs, two of which closed on the *Staffel* leader in a pincer movement. Beckmann's wingman, Sgt Karl-Heinz Klempau, was already suspended from his parachute, his Messerschmitt having been shot down over the High Eifel. Now Lieut Beckmann's G-14 was hit in the rudder, and he too had to reach for his rip-cord. However I Squadron only lost two killed, one of whom, Sgt Sauter, was despatched by Flight Lieutenant Fox of 412 Squadron (Spitfires) near Rheine airfield.

Around 1300 Thunderbolts of 9th US TAF and RAF Tempests of No 486 Squadron came upon a German fighter formation east of Münster, and for the first time in quite a while elements of III *Gruppe*, 54 *Jagdgeschwader*, found themselves in action. It was Lieut Crump's 10 *Staffel* and 1st Lieut Dortenmann's 11 *Staffel*. Straightaway the British picked on the 'long-nosed' FW190s and shot down four aircraft from 10 *Staffel* for the loss of one Tempest, the four kills being credited to Flying Officers Tanner, Taylor-Cannon, Smith and Short.

Generally speaking the American 9th TAF seemed to be out in strength again that day, their Thunderbolts being involved in almost every contact. It even came about that No 137 Squadron's Typhoons were set upon by an American fighter formation, but this scrap ended without loss. With its continuous ground support operations of December 26th and 27th, 9th US TAF played no small part in the defeat of the Ardennes offensive. On these two days 9th TAF recorded 70 kills for a loss of 39 twin-engined bombers, most of them shot down by German AA.

3(Udet) *Geschwader* on the other hand was having a costly day. I, III and IV *Gruppe* were involved between Cologne and the Ahr Hills with American and British fighters which were lurking there in force. Some of this fighting overlapped the action of 1 *Jagdgeschwader* whose squadrons were over the Eifel at the same time but rather further to the south. 14 *Staffel* lost its leader when Lieut Glaubig went down in his 'Black 9' near Antweiler, the victim of a small group of Thunderbolts. And two other Focke-Wulfs of his *Staffel* went the same way. IV *Gruppe*, 3 *Jagdgeschwader*, finished the day with five pilots lost. III *Gruppe's* figure was the same.

On December 27th the 'St Vith operational area', of widespread and ill-repute, did not confine itself to claiming a further toll from 27 *Jagdgeschwader*. Elements of II *Gruppe*, 77 *Geschwader*, and IV *Gruppe*, 54 *Geschwader* which were attached to the main force, also felt the Allied fighter-bombers' deadly sting. 3 pilots from 14 *Staffel*, 54 *Geschwader*, failed to return to their base at Vörden and were reported missing.

Fighter losses on December 27th, 1944

Units taking part	Killed/ missing	Wounded	Total pers/cas	Aircraft	Locality
I./JG1	9	3	12	FW190 A-8	Bastogne,
II./JG1	1	1	2	FW190 A-8	Dinant-Vielsalm,
III./JG1	1		1	Me109 G-14	Mayen,
			—		Munstereifel
			15		
II./JG2		2	2	Me109 G-14	Bruhl
I./JG3	3		3	Me109 G-10/G-14	Antweiler, Liege
III./JG3	4	1	5	Me109 G-14	Malmedy,
IV./JG3	5		5	FW190 A-8/A-9	Marche, St. Vith
			13		
I./JG27	2	1	3	Me109 G-14/K-4	Bastogne,
II./JG27	2	1	3	Me109 G-10/G-14	High Eifel,
IV./JG27	1	1	2	Me109 G-10	Rheine, St. Vith
			8		
III./JG53		1	1	Me109 G-14	Kirrlach,
IV./JG53		1	1	Me109 G-14	Schonaich
			2		
III./JG54	3	2	5	FW190 D-9	Munster, Telgte
IV./JG54	4		4	FW190 A-8	St. Vith, High Eifel
II./JG77	1		1	Me109 G-14	Eupen, St. Vith
Total losses (Germany and Western Theatre)	36	14	50	(incl 1 *Gruppe* commander and 4 *Staffel* leaders killed or missing)	

27 *Jagdgeschwader* alone marked up 10 more kills on December 27th. But although the air battle did not always look hopeless and few chances were missed to give the enemy a bloody nose, the duel in the sky was sheer hell for

most of the German fighter pilots. Many of the wingmen found it more and more difficult and often impossible to cover their formation leader in a tight dogfight. And many leaders were no longer in a position to keep an eye on the green pilots and stop them making ill-considered moves in the heat of battle.

Groundstaff too, the riggers and fitters on the airfields, were stretched to the limit and beyond, and one began to wonder how long they could carry on. Their devotion to duty never got a mention in the operational reports, but they were working continuously right round the clock.

But what was the use of it all? In the last analysis the enemy's overwhelming strength was increasingly calling the tune.

Black Friday

III *Gruppe*, 54 *Jagdgeschwader*, was operating from an airfield on the Cloppenburg-Friesoythe railway line just northeast of the village of Varrelbusch. That Friday every available machine stood ready for the first *Gruppe*-level operation since December 25th when this unit had officially been placed under command of 26 *Geschwader*. In all, almost 70 Focke-Wulf 190 D-9s were to take over take-off and landing cover for the Me262s of 51 *Kampfgeschwader* (Fighters)* based at Rheine. Together with elements of 6 *Jagdgeschwader* from the Oldenburg area and a *Staffel* from IV *Gruppe*, 27 *Jagdgeschwader*, from Achmer, III *Gruppe*, 54 *Jagdgeschwader*, was ordered to take on all low-flying enemy aircraft astride the Dortmund-Ems and Mittelland Canals. 3 *Jagddivision* Group at Wiedenbrück was to provide radio direction ('Y-Führung')†. This was to prove the last major operation for which III *Gruppe*, 54 *Jagdgeschwader*, would take to the air. For the express order from *Jagddivision* control centre to commit the *Gruppe* by *Staffeln* proved completely misguided, with the result that the whole operation failed and ended in catastrophe—just as the *Staffel* leaders had predicted. Seventeen pilots were killed and three injured: it was a Black Friday indeed for III *Gruppe*, 54 *Jagdgeschwader*.

First into the air, at about 0900, was 1st Lieut crump with his 10 *Staffel*. 9, 11 and 12 *Staffeln* followed at intervals of about an hour. One thing which is not clear is why the fighter pilots were not properly briefed on the actual air situation and the real strength of the enemy fighters. For as they were approaching the area of operations, numerous enemy fighter formations were dominating the airspace over the Tecklenburg area and the whole of Münsterland. Under these circumstances it was a serious command error to send units into the air flight by flight and so present the enemy with a chance to intercept them one at a time and destroy them in detail. The problem may have been that certain ground control centres tended not to react on the scale the situation called for and to direct the course of operations speedily enough for the formation commander in the air, who had to read the situation instantly

* See note on p. 61

† VHF R/T ground-air control with Wireless Set FuG 16 ZY (38.5–42.3 Mcs band). The ground station measured the slant range to the airborne transmitter and thus determined the accurate location of friendly aircraft. These figures were processed together with the location and height of the enemy units, so that the fighters could be directed onto the enemy with precision. Conversely, of course, friendly aircraft could be guided back to their various bases ('air defence fighter net'—'Reichsjägerwelle').

and take split-second decisions. And this air defence operation of December 29th 1944 was clearly no exception.

Just as the second sub-unit to go, 9 *Staffel*, reached the area Lingen —Rheine, they were taken by surprise by the Spitfires of 411 Squadron, flying from Heesch in Holland. The German pilots in their Focke-Wulfs barely had time to defend themselves. The flight leader, Lieut Heilmann did everything he could to get his pilots up above the altitude of only 6,500 feet that had been ordered. Six pilots killed and many parachute jumps—no wonder the squadron commander, Capt Weiss, stared helplessly out over the field as, instead of the 9 *Staffel* he expected, only the odd machine came in. It didn't take him long to make up his mind. He took off with his command vic for the operational zone to find out the situation for himself. 11 *Staffel* too was now airborne, with Lieut Prager standing in as its leader.

About noon, with the Dortmund-Ems canal on the starboard hand, the FW190s were closing map-square 'Foxtrot-Quebec' when suddenly a large formation of Spitfires came into view. This time the Germans were able to use their height and dive on the enemy; but then some Typhoon formations appeared out of nowhere down below the Spitfires, and the Germans were heavily outnumbered. A dogfight developed over Lengerich, near Lingen, and ended in WO Neersen and 1st Lieut Schreiner being shot down. In the course of it the squadron commander, Capt Weiss, Knight's Cross, was also killed in a scrap with several Spitfires. By this time 11 *Staffel* had become widely scattered, and its aircraft were hunted down and forced to give battle to the enemy fighters.

The enemy forces involved, 331 and 401 Squadrons with Spitfires and 168 and 439 Squadrons (Typhoons), reported a total of nine confirmed kills and two probables for a loss of six aircraft.

Influenced by what had gone before, 1st Lieut Dortenmann's 12 *Staffel* scrambled from Varrelbusch and climbed straight to 20,000 feet. It was about noon when these further 12 FW190 D-9s set course for Münster and made contact between the Dümmersee and the Ems, most probably with the Tempests of 3 and 56 Squadrons flying from Volkel. In this encounter the flight lost only one pilot, Sgt Seibert, while Sgt Zessin baled out wounded from his 'Red 12'. The evidence strongly suggests that 7 *Staffel* of 6 *Jagdgeschwader* was also involved, for the British shot down Sgt Schneider's A-8 near Wallenhorst. The two British units together lost four Tempests; WO Steinkamp of 13 *Staffel*, 27 *Jagdgeschwader* scored a double, and one further kill was credited to 11 *Staffel*.

Since the parts played in the day's operations by fighter units of both sides frequently overlapped and fighting continued almost uninterrupted from 0900 to 1500, it is impossible to say precisely which units were opposed to one another. Although one can determine in broad terms which units were involved and which made or may have made contact with one another, the operational area was too widespread to be sure that other units were not also involved in a particular engagement. On top of this comes the problem—one which does not only apply to December 29th—that gaps and errors in detailed reporting led to misunderstandings; and these in turn make a proper evaluation of debriefing reports and other documentation extremely difficult. The Allies were apt to apply a pretty broad brush to their location reports, so that for instance 'in the

Enschede area' may well in fact mean 'over the Teutoburger Wald'. In the absence of an opportunity to reconstruct the course of events by means of matching statements and other supporting evidence, this lack of precise locations may significantly distort a detailed account of this kind. Again, it was not only the German pilots who were subject to optical illusions in the matter of aircraft recognition. With FW190s and Me109s alongside each other in almost every encounter, a British or American pilot might well report a kill on a Focke-Wulf instead of a Messerschmitt; likewise the Germans could not always tell Spitfires, Typhoons and Tempests apart, and in the heat of battle they could hardly be expected to. Thus one can only seek to establish whether the total kills and losses can be matched up.

On this basis, the balance-sheet for the operations of December 29th reads as follows. For a loss of 11 fighters, 2 TAF scored 31 kills in all, 5 of them going to Flight Lieutenant Audet of 411 Squadron. German reports give a loss of 20 aircraft from 627 and 54 *Jagdgeschwadern*; but the lost machines of pilots who baled out unwounded must be added to these, so there is no reason to doubt the enemy figures.

In any event the German Air Force took a painful blow, for the losses amounted to roughly a third of the aircraft committed—a sacrifice which could have been avoided by better operational planning. But the most severe loss of the day was without doubt the death of a battle-hardened formation leader, the 24-year-old Capt Robert Weiss, who had commanded III *Gruppe* 54 *Jagdgeschwader*, since July 1944 and had 121 kills to his credit.

No New Year Celebration
On December 30th, US 8th Air Force heavy bombers had raided communications centres round Kasselm, Mannheim and Kaiserslautern, and now it was the fuel industry's turn. This last day of 1944, a rugged year of war, saw yet another major air battle in the North German skies—a battle which cost the Americans 39 heavy bombers and I *Jagdgeschwader* 20 pilots killed, 4 missing and 10 wounded. Among the German casualties were one *Gruppe* commander and 2 *Staffel* leaders, and the loss of these experienced men struck home hard.

The bomber force of some 1,300 machines flew in over North Germany with the Hamburg-Harburg refineries and the hydrogenation plant at Misburg as its targets; it need scarcely be said that an escort of several fighter groups accompanied the Flying Fortresses. This massive incursion was faced by the 'home team' of 300 and 301 *Jagdgeschwader*, with a total of 14 *Staffel*. Two *Staffel* had Me109s and the rest FW190 A-8s, A-9s and the odd D-9, a total of 150–190 machines of which at least 40 were to be lost.

Headquarters III *Gruppe* and 10 *Staffel*, 300 *Jagdgeschwader*, hoped to intercept the bombers around Langenhagen to the north of Hanover; but the Messerschmitts met the enemy fighter escort instead. The battle that followed cost III *Gruppe* the life of its commander, Major Hans-Karl Kamp, his machine with the command chevrons on its fuselage being shot down in flames.

Meanwhile I *Jagddivsion* had scrambled the whole of II *Gruppe*, 300 *Jagdgeschwader* (the assault *Gruppe*) and ordered them to close on map-square 'Delta-Tango' from the south, dead ahead of the leading formations of the mighty stream of bombers. As they were going into a frontal attack, the speck-led grey Focke-Wulfs with the red-brown band of home air defence on their fuselages were taken from above by the fighter escort. The 'air battle of Roten-burg' was under way. But one American bomber after another went down; the lead formation, 3rd Air Division, itself lost 14 B 17s, half of them from 100th Bombardment Group; and the Hamburg AA artillery accounted for 10 more.

But this duel to the death over Rotenburg, near Bremen, took its toll of the German fighter force too. The first two assault fighters to go were shot down near Unterstedt, to the southwest of Rotenburg; 7 and 8 *Staffeln* each reported one pilot missing, quite possibly after crashing into the peatbogs of Borschels-moor or Great Lohmoor.

It was US 78th and 364th Fighter Groups who made things most difficult for the German fighters as they tried to stick with the bombers and go on shooting them down. But meanwhile all three squadrons of 301 *Jagdgeschwader* were flying in from the Salzwedel area, and elements of them soon reached the battle area and joined in. They too scored some kills on the heavy bombers, but them-selves lost four machines including the 'Red 19' flown by 10 *Staffel* leader, 1st Lieut Stahl.

The other formations simply never got through to the Rotenburg area, being intercepted and pinned down by the Americans and losing three more 301 *Jagd-geschwader* pilots killed in the process.

The battle formed a second focus on the right flank of the bomber forma-tions, southeast of Hamburg. There, astride the Elbe, American fighters in strength blocked off the attack by 6, 8, 11 and 12 *Staffel*, 301 *Jagdgeschwader*. At about the same time the Flying Fortresses, their bomb-doors already open, turned sharply to the northwest and ran in on their target. When 1st Lieut Herzog led his 11 *Staffel* off from Stendal that morning, he can scarcely have imagined that he was about to lose four pilots. 11 *Staffel* crossed the big bend of the Elbe at Hitzacker and pressed on towards the Hamburg-Berlin railway line, where they came face to face with the Americans.

In ones and twos the Germans went on trying to follow the bomber forma-tion, which had meanwhile vanished into the midday haze and was headed for home. This pursuit cost 10 *Staffel* yet another casualty, the Americans shooting down Lieut Max Müller near Stade. Thus 10 and 11 *Staffel* lost four pilots each on December 31st—6 killed, one missing and one wounded.

But apart from a few tactical missions, the bulk of the German air defence fighter units stayed on the ground on December 31st; every available machine was required for the large-scale fighter operation planned for the following day—a special task of which only a very few pilots had an inkling. 6 *Staffel*, 1 *Jagdgeschwader*, for instance, were still smarting from a skirmish with Typhoons from 137 Squadron RAF, in which three of their pilots had been killed in action over Emsdetten and Mesum. During the morning Spitfires from 411, 416 and 422 Squadrons were again making things hot over Münsterland, where they encountered about 15 Messerschmitts, probably from III *Gruppe* 27 *Jagdgeschwader*. The British went straight in and scored four kills.

Sector Control Middle Rhine at Darmstadt had scrambled two flights of 4

Jagdgeschwader from the Rhine-Main area and directed them into the Palatinate to counter American fighter-bombers. This operation cost 16 *Staffel* two lives—1st Lieut Hans Schleef, the flight leader, with at least 98 kills to his credit, and Sgt Klein.

When at last the roar of battle faded from the skies and the BMW, Jumo and Daimler-Benz engines were silent, many a pilot was drawing up a mental balance-sheet. One does not know the outcome of their ponderings; no doubt their differing approaches, outlooks, imaginations and powers of expression led to a whole variety of answers. But it is safe to assume that the question in the forefront of their minds was whether their game was any longer worth the candle. Nor can one tell how many gave way to such thoughts. After the long weeks of bitter, hopeless struggle, many a fighter pilot was looking forward to celebrating New Year's Eve 1945 by looking on the wine when it was red and so forgetting for a few hours at least the futility and the horror of it all, the daily toll in lives and the uncertainty over his own fate—to drowning his sorrows in fact. They were certainly in for a rude shock.

Early in the evening all passes were cancelled and all drink was forbidden. Before them stood the most demanding, sweeping operation to be flown by German fighter pilots in the whole of the War, and one that was to prove the costliest—Operation Baseplate!

Fighter losses on December 31st, 1944

Units taking part	Killed/ missing	Wounded	Total pers/cas	Aircraft	Locality
II./JG1	3	1	4	FW190 A-8	Emsdetten, Mesum
I./JG2	1		1	FW190 D-9	Coblenz
III./JG4	2		2	Me109 K-4	Bad Durkheim,
IV./JG4	2		2	Me109 G-14	Bastogne, Eisenberg
			4		
I./JG6	1		1	FW190 A-8	Oldenzaal
III./JG54		1	1	FW109 D-9	Limburg
IV./JG54	1		1	FW190 A-8	Osnabruck, Munster
III./JG77	3		3	Me109 K-4	Hemer, Munster
II./JG300	6	3	9	FW190 A-8	Altenhorst, Hoya
III./JG300	2		2	Me109 G-10	Rotenburg, Unterstedt
			11		
I./JG301	1	3	4	FW190 A-9/R 11	Boitzenburg,
II./JG301	7	1	8	FW190 A-9/R 11	Fassberg,
III./JG301	8	3	11	FW190 A-8	Luneberg, Riepe, Soltau
			23		
Total losses (Germany and Western Theatre)	37	12	49	(incl 1 *Gruppe* commander and 3 *Staffel* leaders killed, 1 *Gruppe* commander and 2 *Staffel* leaders wounded)	

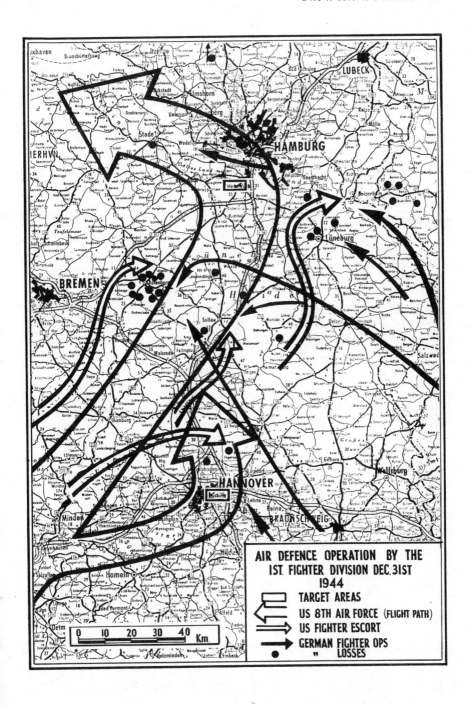

AIR DEFENCE OPERATION BY THE
1ST. FIGHTER DIVISION DEC. 31ST
1944
TARGET AREAS
US 8TH AIR FORCE (FLIGHT PATH)
US FIGHTER ESCORT
GERMAN FIGHTER OPS
„ LOSSES

Review of December

Even more than the preceding month, the past weeks had demonstrated the British and American pilots' superior mastery of operational flying in the foulest of weathers. The result was, that on most days of December the home air defence fighter pilots were again faced with superior numbers wherever they turned.

Moreover the enemy succeeded in gaining not only the initiative on the fronts but along with it control of the rear areas; as a result the month was marked by disruption of the communications system and destruction of air force installations. Thus in this last month of 1944, in bombing raids on as many as 80 airfields, 129 machines were destroyed on the ground and a further 140 damaged. In the last four days of the month the Allied air forces flew 5,500 heavy bomber sorties over Germany; I *Jagdkorps* shot down 63 bombers and 23 escort fighters for the loss of 128 fighters. In the same period, according to Major-General Grabmann, AA artillery accounted for almost three times as many enemy aircraft. It follows that the German day-fighters could no longer be claimed to offer an effective defence.

The losses were devastating. From the beginning of the month to the opening of the German Ardennes offensive on December 16th, 136 fighter pilots failed to return. In the four days from December 19th to 22nd, the figure was 'only' 83. But in the week or so from December 23rd to 31st the fighter units lost 316 pilots killed or missing, quite apart from the wounded. Over Christmas alone, *Luftflotte* Headquarters West and the units attached to it for the Ardennes offensive suffered over 260 aircrew casualties. On these figures it would appear that German fighter force casualties for December 1944 amounted to 500 pilots killed or missing, 35 taken prisoner and 194 wounded.

In face of attrition on this scale, it is remarkable to say the least that Operation Baseplate, planned for New Year's Day, could take place at all. But, as few would now gainsay, the outcome of the War had long since been decided. It was of little help that the *Luftwaffe* High Command at last seemed to have appreciated that the *Luftwaffe* was no longer capable of influencing the course of events. The fighter pilots had become a forlorn hope, and their outstanding achievements will probably never receive the credit they deserve.

III *Dawn Scramble*

Operation Baseplate
January 1st, 1945

When the fighters' 'Big Punch' planned for early November never came to fruition and the forces initially intended for it were cut to pieces supporting the Ardennes offensive, that seemed to be the end of the matter. Few people indeed still believed in the possibility of a mass operation by the Luftwaffe. But towards the end of December Headquarters II *Jagdkorps* received a directive ordering them to mount a large-scale operation, to be carried out in the early morning of a day as yet unnamed. All available day fighters were to be committed to low-level attacks on the Allied air forces' infrastructure in Holland, Belgium and France. The intention of Luftwaffe Headquarters Germany was effectively to take out the enemy fighter force based on the Continent. They saw this as the only way to break the Allied fighter superiority once and for all and thus to regain a position from which to mount a more effective defence against the bomber hordes. The aim of the operation was then: to regain control of Western airspace, lost since the Allied landings.

The plan for Operation Baseplate, one of the most controversial in the history of the German fighter force, can only have been born of desperation. Pilots were sent into an operation which failed to achieve its aim—and was bound to fail, for the fighter force had already been bled dry. For months the pilots had felt themselves misjudged and had had to carry this moral burden through their hopeless battles. To begin with it was Hitler who, faced with streams of enemy bombers pouring unhindered into Germany, repeatedly questioned the operational fitness of the fighter defence. Then the Commander-in-Chief of the Luftwaffe weighed in with his accusations, which culminated in his announcing that the fighter force was manned entirely by cowards.

Göring's first meeting with the commanders of the day and night fighter forces at the beginning of November had borne little fruit. One side demanded greater efforts and better results, while the other—for the thousandth time —tried to put across the facts which underlay the real reasons for the 'failures'—inadequate pilot reinforcements, lack of equipment and spares, and *Jagdgeschwadern* incredibly understrength.

True, the fighter men's appeal did not go wholly unheard. But the repeatedly called-for major and decisive operation amounted in fact to the senseless frittering away in penny packets, in battles over Germany and the Western theatre, of the resources assembled for it. Back in autumn 1944 a massive counterstroke of the kind envisaged by Galland would indeed have stood a very good chance of succeeding. The estimated loss of as many as 400 of our own aircraft was seen as acceptable provided that at least the same number of bombers was destroyed. But in the meantime the losses in home air defence units had risen far above this figure without making any sensible impression on the enemy. And by the time 1944 drew to its close the moment for the 'Big Punch' was long past.

Yet it was only then that the Luftwaffe High Command, reacting like a wounded stag at bay, concocted a plan intended to change the situation at a stroke, a carefully drawn-up plan but one that was finally to tear the heart out of the remnants of the fighter force—Operation Baseplate. Appointed to lead it was Major-General Peltz. As commander of II *Jagdkorps* he was responsible for air operations in the Ardennes offensive, thus usurping the role of General Galland, Director of Fighters, who had been placed in cold storage.

A spell of bad weather having been deliberately chosen for the launching of the Army's counter-offensive, there was no choice but to hold the Air Force's operation over until the weather cleared. This happened towards the end of December. The plan lay under extreme security restrictions, but the small band of the initiated knew that Baseplate was to take place in the early morning of January 1st, 1945.

Even today it is still widely supposed that the morning of New Year's Day was chosen for the operation simply because it was hoped that the general celebrations would impair the alertness of the enemy defence. Although this factor could not but operate in the undertaking's favour, the supposition was in fact a false one. Choice of the date for Baseplate was based wholly on the weather, and Monday, January 1st, 1945 happened to be the first occasion on which conditions were suitable.

The outline plan for Baseplate had already come up at the December meeting of all *Jagddivision* commanders concerned. 'Under complete wireless silence up to the moment of attacking,*all wings will fly low over the frontier simultaneously in the early hours of the morning, to take the enemy air forces by surprise and catch them on the ground.' Outward and return flight paths were laid down and all relevant navigational data was entered on the pilots' operation maps—but only the other side of the German frontier, so that if a marked map fell into enemy hands, the bases of the various units could not be directly identified.

'Wings will receive air photos of the targets allotted to them and will use these at their briefings to take every pilot through the operation in detail.' Thus the II *Jagdkorps* directive. But such meticulous preparation was not always achieved, for to prevent the enemy learning of the operation in advance most briefings were not held until just before take-off and, in the short time available, many commanders were happy if they managed to get the bare essentials across to their pilots. When Baseplate got under way, there were still many who did not know what it was all about. They were thinking in terms of a reconnaissance in force over the front line or were content just to follow their leader.

So the fighter pilots got their instructions in briefings that ranged from the

---

* In fact it appears that wireless silence was imposed until return to base. (Tr)

Organisation on 1st January 1945
(Operation Baseplate)
Luftflotte Headquarters West (Schmid)
Limburg
II *Jagdkorps* (Peltz)
Flammersfeld

3 *Jagddivision* (Grabmann)	*No of Gruppen*	*Targets allotted*
WIEDENBRUCK		
1 *Jagdgeschwader*	3	St. Denis-Westrem (Belgium)
3 *Jagdgeschwader*	3	Eindhoven (Holland)
6 *Jagdgeschwader*	3	Volkel (Holland)
26 *Jagdgeschwader*	3	Btussels-Evère (Belgium)
with under command		
III *Gruppe*, 54 *Geschwader*	1	Brussels-Grimbergen (Belgium)
27 *Jagdgeschwader*	4	Brussels-Melsbroek (Belgium)
with under command		
IV *Gruppe*, 54 *Geschwader*	1	
77 *Geschwader*	3	Antwerp-Deurne (Belgium)

Middle Rhine Fighter Sector (Handrick)

DARMSTADT		
2 *Jagdgeschwader*	3	St. Trond (Belgium)
4 *Jagdgeschwader*	3	Le Culot (Belgium)
11 *Jagdgeschwader*	3	Asch (Belgium)

5 *Jagddivision* (Hentschel)

KARLSRUHE		
53 *Jagdgeschwader*	3	Metz-Frescaty (France)

Elements of the following units also took part in the operation:
Special flight, 104 *Jagdgeschwader*   (under command 26 *Jagdgeschwader*
4 Close Support *Geschwader*   (under command 2 *Jagdgeschwader*
20 Independent Night Close Support
Gruppe
51 *Kampfgeschwader* (Fighters)

Sources indicate that the pathfinder aircraft were drawn from the following night fighter units among others:

5 Flight, 1 Night *Jagdgeschwader*
7 Flight, 1 Night *Jagdgeschwader*
9 Flight, 1 Night *Jagdgeschwader*
4 Flight, 3 Night *Jagdgeschwader*
9 Flight, 3 Night *Jagdgeschwader*
10 Flight, 3 Night *Jagdgeschwader*
11 Squadron, 101 Night *Jagdgeschwader*

sparse in detail to, in a few instances, extravagant exhortations aimed at boosting morale by recalling the heroic fighter tradition, and by references to Führer and country and to what the German people expected of them. But these fighter pilots had already given of their best in courage and readiness to sacrifice themselves. The commanders who gave vent to such pathetic appeals either had not been on the operations of Christmas 1944 or happened to be giving their briefing in a higher headquarters ops room. Or perhaps they deliberately tried that January morning to paint their pilots a false picture.

In fact the pilots' morale was impressively high—far higher than could be expected after weeks of hard fighting and heavy casualties. In all units most of the men showed high confidence; the younger and less experienced in particular were enthusiastic about the plan and were convinced that they would be just as successful in taking the enemy by surprise and inflicting a damaging blow as their ground forces had been on December 16th. They were not to know that the success of two weeks back had almost played itself out and that today's operation was doomed to failure before it even started. They had no real idea of the broader picture and, as always, underestimated the enemy. It is true that never before that January morning had so many fighters stood on the tarmac ready for take-off—but the bottom of the barrel had been scraped. In fact some 900*aircraft stood waiting to carry the German fighter force on its flight to destruction.

One or two night fighters were allotted to each wing to guide it on a prearranged course over the front lines. These pathfinder aircraft then turned away and did not themselves take part in the operation. And the pilots received one other important instruction: 'Look out for 'golden rain''.' This referred to marker flares used as additional navigational aids for the fighter pilots and to warn ground troops and the forward area AA artillery†of a low-level flight across the front by our own fighters. But the use of 'golden rain' was planned mainly for the area of the Middle Rhine Fighter Sector.

'But what will happen if the golden rain doesn't work for some reason or other? What if our AA gunners don't know it's us over their heads? Whoever asked this question can scarcely have guessed that it would provide the heading for a tragic chapter in the history of the German fighter force.

German AA was to play a disastrous part in Baseplate and, unintentionally of course, to make a substantial contribution to our fighter losses. At the turn of 1944/45 *Luftflotte* Headquarters West had under its command about 267 heavy and 277 medium or light AA batteries, and in addition to this there were 100 naval AA batteries on the Dutch North Sea coast. The path of most of the attacking formations lay over the sector of 16 AA Division, with its fire control centre at Doetinchem some 15 miles east of Arnhem. This AA formation, commanded by Major-General Deutsch, was over 50 batteries strong.

Again, the Baseplate briefing had said: 'To achieve maximum surprise the

---

* Feuchter quotes a figure of 800. Allied estimates put the number of machines taking part as 790–870, while the Supreme Headquarters operations log for January 1st, 1945 gives a total of 1,035. (Author)

† This distinction is drawn because in the German Armed Forces structure of the time the AA artillery formed part of the Air Force (or in certain cases of the Navy). (Tr.)

plan is to attack all target airfields simultaneously, or as near simultaneously as possible'—an instruction that unfortunately did not quite work out and thus paved the way for a disaster.

16 AA Division was indeed informed of the operation, but the passage of information was totally inadequate. Only a fraction of the batteries knew the times at which the German fighters were due to overfly their positions and free-firing areas. And then, when for one reason or another—a sudden groundmist on the field, having to wait for their pathfinders, or delays in forming up—the take-off of some wings or squadrons was delayed, nobody thought to pass the revised timings to the AA gunners. When strong fighter forces approached at the wrong times, the gunners took them for enemy and let fly at them. The results were catastrophic. Any aircraft that the enemy didn't manage to shoot down were pulled out of the sky by our own batteries—to the tune, it is estimated, of about 100 machines.

But this still lay in the future. Now ten *Jagdgeschwadern* with a total of 33 *Gruppen* were standing waiting for the order to go. Under every machine hung a 65 gallon jettison-tank. Just before take-off the pilots received their final orders: 'Mission Hermann, 1.1.1945, time 0920.'

The codeword 'Hermann' signified time of attack and this therefore meant that all units were to go into the attack on the enemy airfields at twenty past nine.

The weather in the operational area was more or less as forecast; by and large the sky was clear to overcast, with rather heavier cloud cover over the Belgium-Dutch border; visibility was ideal and the pilots had no need to worry about rain. But despite this the operation did not get under way on time; in many areas, especially in north-west Germany, an unexpected groundmist suddenly came up, causing delays in take-off with the disastrous consequences described above.

But even if this large-scale operation did not always achieve the hoped-for degree of surprise, the Allies could scarcely have reckoned with a mass attack by the Luftwaffe, least of all on New Year's morning 1945. The Luftwaffe succeeded in causing considerable confusion and inflicting substantial damage, most of all in the 2nd TAF area, that is in the British sector of the front. Many of the British, and of the Americans too, were at that first moment hardly in a state to produce an instant defensive reaction. But as the first shock wore off, strong and increasing counter-action on their part weakened or frustrated every low-level attack. It was not until after the end of the War that the Germans fully realised that a number of Allied airfields—including some of those listed as primary targets such as Antwerp, Le Culot or Volkel—were untouched or were engaged only by a few machines. Other fields, among them Knocke and Ophoven, were attacked during Operation Baseplate, because they were listed as secondary targets or were mistaken for the allotted target. And thanks to inadequate aerial reconnaissance it happened on occasion that a strong fighter force attacked an airfield, Grimbergen for instance, only to find it unoccupied except for a few machines.

There are conflicting data on the losses suffered by the enemy that New Year's morning. The British figures are 144 Allied aircraft destroyed and 84 damaged, while American sources report 134 total losses and 62 damaged beyond repair. These figures look very low and may well in fact represent not the overall losses by those in 2nd TAF and 9th US TAF areas respectively.

The German Air Force High Command report on Baseplate, dated January 27th, 1945, states that photo-reconnaissance of eight airfields showed 279 machines destroyed on the ground (239 single-engined, 21 twin-engined and 19 four-engined). This probably does not tell the whole story, and on top of it the German fighters shot down 65–75 enemy aircraft. Thus visual reconnaissance reports on seven other airfields give a total of 123 machines (113 single-engined). The above figures do not include the 114 damaged aircraft observed on all these airfields together.

The inescapable point is that the Allies lost five hundred aircraft at a stroke —a loss that they were certainly able to make good in something under a fort-night. And it caused scarcely a ripple in Allied aircrew strength. For the Luft-waffe it was a very different story.

Details of German losses follow the accounts of individual units' parts in the operation.

Name of Airfield		Allied Code No	Effectiveness of Attack*
Antwerp-Deurne	(Belgium)	B-70	3
Asch	(Belgium)	Y-29	2
Brussels-Evère	(Belgium)	B-56	1
Brussels-Grimbergen	(Belgium)	B-60	2
Brussels-Melsbroek	(Belgium)	B-58	1
Eindhoven	(Holland)	B-78	1
Ghent/St-Denis-Westrem	(Belgium)	B-61	1
Gilze-Rijen	(Holland)	B-77	4
Heesch	(Holland)	B-88	4
Knocke	(Belgium)		4
Le Culot	(Belgium)	A-89	3
Maldegem	(Belgium)	B-65	1
Metz-Frescaty	(France)	Y-34	2
Ophoven	(Belgium)	Y-32	4
St Trond	(Belgium)	A-92	2
Volkel	(Holland)	B-80	3
Woensdrecht	(Holland)	B-79	4
Ursel	(Belgium)	B-67	3
and probably			
Beauvechain	(Belgium)		
Helmond	(Holland)		
Grave	(Holland)		

*1 = successful
2 = moderately successful
3 = not attacked/only intermittently attacked
4 = attacked by mistake/as opportunity target. No effect.

Allied Aircraft losses caused by Operation Baseplate

Source	Destroyed on ground	Shot down	Total destroyed	+ Damaged
GERMAN				
Armed Forces communique 2.1.45	400	79	479	100
Situation report 2.1.45			507	
Luftwaffe High Command Report 27.1.45	402	65 (+12)	467 (+12)	114
Bartz, Clostermann, Feuchter			80	
Galland			400	
ALLIED				
RAF (2 TAF)			144	84
USAAF			⎰196	
			⎱150*	50

*30 USAAF, 120 RAF.

Bases of II Jagdkorps Units taking part in operation Baseplate

Unit/Sub-Unit	Aircraft	Location
1 *Jagdgeschwader*		
I *Gruppe*	FW190 A-8	Twenthe
II *Gruppe*	FW190 A-8	Drope
III *Gruppe*	Me109 G-14	Rheine
2 *Jagdgeschwader*		
I *Gruppe*	FW190 A-8/A-9	Merzhausen
II *Gruppe*	Me109 G-14/K-4	Nidda, Ettingshausen
III *Gruppe*	FW190 D-9	Altenstadt
3 *Jagdgeschwader*		
I *Gruppe*	Me109 G-10/G-14	Paderborn
III *Gruppe*	Me109 G-14/K-4	Lippspringe
IV *Gruppe*	FW190 A-8	Gutersloh
4 *Jagdgeschwader*		
I *Gruppe*	Me190 G-14/K-4	Darmstadt-Greisheim
II *Gruppe*	FW190 A-8	Babenhausen
IV *Gruppe*	Me109 G-14/K-4	Rhine-Main
6 *Jagdgeschwader*		
I *Gruppe*	FW190 A-8	Delmenhorst
II *Gruppe*	FW190 A-8	Quakenbruck, Vechta
III *Gruppe*	Me109 G-10/G-14	Bissel

11 *Jagdgeschwader*

I *Gruppe*	FW109 A-8	Darmstadt-Greisheim
II *Gruppe*	Me109 G-14/K-4	Zellhausen
III *Gruppe*	FW190 A-8	Gross-Ostheim

26 *Jagdgeschwader*

I *Gruppe*	FW190 D-9	Furstenau
II *Gruppe*	FW190 D-9	Nordhorn
III *Gruppe*	Me109 G-14/K-4	Plantlunne

27 *Jagdgeschwader*

I *Gruppe*	Me109 G-14/K-4	Rheine
II *Gruppe*	Me109 G-14	Rheine
III *Gruppe*	Me109 K-4	Hesepe
IV *Gruppe*	Me109 G-10	Achmer

53 *Jagdgeschwader*

II *Gruppe*	Me109 G-14/K-4	Malmsheim
III *Gruppe*	Me109 G-14	Kirrlach
IV *Gruppe*	Me109 G-14	St.-Echterdingen

54 *Jagdgeschwader*

III *Gruppe*	FW190 D-9	Furstenau
IV *Gruppe*	FW190 A-8/A-9	Vorden

77 *Jagdgeschwader*

I *Gruppe*	Me109 G-14	Dortmund
II *Gruppe*	Me109 K-4	Bonninghardt
III *Gruppe*	Me109 K-4	Dusseldorf-Lohausen

4 Close Support *Geschwader*

III *Gruppe*	FW190 F-8	Cologne-Wahn

Special *Staffel,*

104 *Jagdgeschwader*	FW190 D-9	Furstenau

20 Independent Night Close

Support *Gruppe*	FW190 F-8/G-3	Bonn-Hangelar

51 *Kampfgeschwader*

(Fighters)	Me262A	Rheine

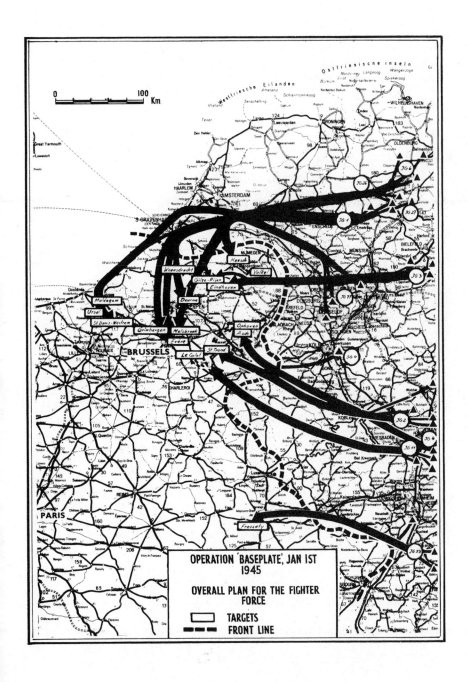

OPERATION 'BASEPLATE', JAN 1ST
1945

OVERALL PLAN FOR THE FIGHTER
FORCE

TARGETS
FRONT LINE

The Suicide Mission of 1 Jagdgeschwader

A bare 10 miles from the German frontier, in the triangle Oldenzaal-Hengelo-Enschede, lies the airfield of Twenthe, which I *Gruppe*, 1(Oesau) *Jagdgeschwader* had shared with Capt Rath's I *Gruppe*, 2 Night Fighter *Jagdgeschwader* since being transferred there in mid-December 1944. On New Year's Eve they still knew no details of the following morning's major operation, but they smelt a rat because everyone was confined to quarters. When Capt Hackbarth gave them the details of Baseplate at his briefing on the morning of January 1st, they felt easier in their minds. At least the outward flight would be safe enough, most of them reckoned, because they would be flying mainly over ground held by their own troops. They were to come in over the sea to attack their target, Maldegem airfield about 10 miles east of Bruges.

Their pathfinders would be two Ju88s from their own *Geschwader*. The first vic was airborne at 0730. There are woods to the east and south of the field, and they swung to port onto the line of the railway and the arrow-straight Hengelo-Oldenzaal road before setting course for the southern tip of the Zuider Zee. They were followed at a few minutes' interval by the Messerschmitts of III *Gruppe* from Rheine, which was to join them in the attack on Maldegem —some 55 aircraft in all, led by Capt Hackbarth in his FW190 A-8 and the rest of I *Gruppe* Headquarters.

However the outward flight was not to prove so easy as they had thought, for the pilots in I *Gruppe's* four *Staffeln* were scarcely to know that the German AA had not been fully briefed on German fighter movements. Large fighter formations like this, especially if they were still flying low in the coastal area, were bound to be hostile—so the gunners reasoned: By the time they realised their mistake, it was in most cases too late.

Sgts Comtesse of 1 *Staffel* and Kilian of 3 *Staffel* were the first to die in this operation; but south of Rotterdam the flak brought down a third machine, 3 *Staffel's* 'Yellow 15'. Its pilot, Sgt Heinz Böhmer, did his best to fly east along the Old Maas and regain friendly territory, but the Focke-Wulf went in at Strijen, about eight miles southeast of Dordrecht. I *Gruppe's* pilots could scarcely contain their anger with their friends in the AA batteries, for they had no idea of the circumstances. At this moment the temptation to break radio silence was great; but they did not break it.

Now they had the North Sea coast just north of the Hague ahead of them; the sea looked leaden and uninviting in the grey light of dawn. In a few minutes the leaders were over the Island of Schouwen; still the enemy did not seem to have spotted them, for there was no sign of defensive action so far. Despite this the whole formation looked rather untidy; losing three pilots had played on their nerves, but fortunately nobody cracked.

Between Blankenberge and Knokke the Focke-Wulfs turned south towards Bruges and then headed east again. Over Bruges five aircraft of 4 *Staffel* broke formation and headed on southwards. 1st Lieut Meinhoff with this tiny force had gone off to see if there were any worthwhile targets on the airstrip some six miles south of Maldegem between Knesselare and Ursel.

Meanwhile the remainder of I *Gruppe* and elements of III *Gruppe* went in to attack Maldegem. They had planned to make five runs, but something went wrong with this idea. It later emerged that in the general confusion a whole bunch of aircraft had without realising it tagged on to II *Gruppe*, which had meanwhile appeared on the scene, and these pilots suddenly found themselves back over the St Denis-Westrem field. III *Gruppe's* Messerschmitts reached Maldegem without interference to find it difficult to spot targets on the ground and so made a strafing run in the hope of hitting something. So it came about that Maldegem did not receive the full weight of the attack; but 11 parked Spitfires of 485 Squadron RAF were set on fire and two others damaged, leaving this squadron with only 5 serviceable aircraft.

After the attack III *Gruppe* turned away to the north to start its homeward flight. The squadron had lost two machines, the pilots being taken prisoner by the British. In a few minutes, they reckoned, they would all be safely back over their own lines. But fate had decided otherwise. No one knows whether WO Wilhelm Kraüter's machine was hit by flak or fell to an enemy fighter; whatever it was may have happened back over Maldegem. Now 'Green 23' suddenly plunged straight down and shattered on the ground near Dirksland on Overflakkee Island.

Neither German nor Allied sources reveal whether the diversionary attack on Ursel was successful. In any event Sgt Fritzsche was shot down by enemy AA before reaching the target and captured by the British. The flight leader, 1st Lieut Meinhoff, also failed to get back to Twenthe. 'Red 8', which he was flying on this sortie, was hit by flak on the way home and crashed, Meinhoff's body being found near Breda.

Just after 0900 the Focke-Wulfs of II *Gruppe* 1 *Jagdgeschwader*, roared in from the southwest over the St Denis-Westrem field. After taking off from Drope, to the north of Rheine, the 30 machines at first followed almost the same flight path as the other two *Gruppen*. Then they broke up into *Staffeln* and flew between the Leie and the Schelde, both these rivers leading them on to the airfield, situated to the south of Ghent. It was a long time since the Flemish had had a sight of a German aircraft, and at first they took them for Spitfire squadrons flying back into St Denis-Westrem after an operation. But the 1 *Jagdgeschwader* pilots knew that their attack would not take the enemy completely by surprise, for the widespread dogfights over the Maldegem area could scarcely have passed unnoticed.

Stationed at St Denis-Westrem were three Polish squadrons of 131 Wing RAF. All three were airborne—in more senses than one—in the early hours of January 1st, 1945. 302 Squadron was the first back in, landing with its tanks almost dry right into its own flak and the hail of bullets from the German fighters' guns. For the German attack went in at the very moment the Spitfires were taxying in or about to touch down. One Spitfire crashed after being hit by flak and the 1 *Geschwader* aircraft destroyed a further nine. Fires blazed up all over the airfield.

Two German fighters went down just near the field.

When the German attack on St Denis-Westrem began, the enemy immediately recalled the two other squadrons. Only a few minutes after the first Spitfires had landed in the German fighters' fire, 308 Squadron was closing the airfield from the northeast. The Polish pilots were about 12 miles from Ghent

NORTH SEA

AMSTERDAM

The Hague

II JG/1

▲ Drone II/JG1

▲ Rheine III/JG 1

Twenthe JG1

Rotterdam

80-82
Bf109 G-14
Fw190 A-8

GERMANY

○ Dortmund

Eindhoven

○ Dusseldorf

Maldegem
Ursel
Gent-St. Denis

Antwerp

○ Cologne

BRUSSELS

○ Aachen

Frankfurt

PARIS
○

○ Mannheim

Metz
○

F R A N C E

○ Karlsruhe

0   50   100
      Km.

ACTION JG1 1.1.45

when they spotted the first Focke-Wulfs over Kokeren and forced four of them to give battle.

As the Spitfires reached their smoke-shrouded base, 1 *Jagdgeschwader* was just making another low-level run. Six parked fighters belonging to 317 Squadron went up in flames; WO Fritz Hofmann of 3 Flight caught another four-engined machine standing on the edge of the field and in that very instant was himself hit by the airfield's light AA. His sortie ended in a prison camp.

The Germans had no time for further runs, for they had their work cut out keeping the Spitfires off their tails. The British were gradually gaining the upper hand, and a vicious dogfight now flared up over Ghent and the rolling plains of East Flanders.

'I must get out!'—a voice suddenly came up loud and clear on the RT; and the pilots in their Focke-Wulfs winced. Those who had not got a dogfight on their hands at the moment tried to spot the machine they presumed to be plunging earthwards. No one seemed to know quite what to do. Was wireless silence still on? The events of the past fifteen minutes had made anything of that kind worse than pointless. No one knew whose mouth had uttered this desperate call or whether the pilot was still in a position to bale out. Only one thing was clear —the number of German machines going down was mounting steadily. Lieut Swoboda's 5 *Staffel* was already down to half strength after losing five pilots.

The two Polish Spitfire pilots Stanowski and Breyner despatched two Focke-Wulfs each, and Flight-Lieutenant Chojnacki, after destroying another FW190, was himself shot down and killed. After a duel over Ghent a Focke-Wulf went down to crash in the riverside depots of the Schelde, but in the heat of battle no one could make out its tactical sign.

At last this mission too was over, one which had cost 'Oesau' *Jugdgeschwader* 24 pilots. Six of them were in Allied hands, and the fate of four remains unresolved. Enemy records show that the wreckage of 19 German aircraft was found in the general area of Ghent. Even though the enemy's losses in material exceeded those of 1 *Jagdgeschwader*, with 32 Spitfires destroyed in all, 18 of them on St Denis-Westrem, his casualties were minimal. Only one pilot each from 308 and 317 Squadrons was killed in action.

Colonel Ihlefeld, commander 1 *Jagdgeschwader*, made no secret of his bitterness. He too had guessed well enough how a desperate throw of this kind was bound to end. There can be no doubt that lack of quality and quantity in pilot reinforcements and over-hasty mounting of the operation were the reasons why, of the 1 *Jagdgeschwader* aircraft which took off on Operation Baseplate, one third was sacrificed to no good purpose.

The End of Richthofen Jagdgeschwader

On the northern slopes of the Taunus, a bare 20 miles as the crow flies from Frankfurt-on-Main and looking south onto the Usingen-Idstein road, lies Merzhausen airfield, where I *Gruppe*, 2(Richthofen) *Jagdgeschwader*, had been stationed since the beginning of October 1944. On January 1st, it was still dark when the pilots of all four *Staffeln* left their billets in Altweilnau, Niederlauken and Wilhelmsdorf on the short journey to the airfield.

The briefing was soon over. The *Staffel* leaders themselves had only been told the target in the small hours, and there was little time left to explain the concept of the operation to the 30 pilots. So the cry was: 'Follow me and stay with me!'

Slowly the trucks càrrying the pilots in their black leather flying-suits pulled onto the airstrip. Feelings were mixed; some were still muttering darkly about missing their New Year's party—despite everything, a few had managed to get a drop or two on board; others seemed more cheerful, even high-spirited. They only realised how this operation was once again going to stretch their flying skill to the limit to the extent that they recalled how every sortie of the past few weeks had turned into a dogfight with no quarter given, in which in the end they had had to resign themselves to the enemy's monstrous superiority. But Baseplate was to exceed their wildest forebodings, although the whole operation could in fact have been a success—if the fighter force had been properly and methodically prepared for it.

In other *Gruppen* the picture was the same; there too the 'couldn't care less' attitude would soon disappear, when just an hour later 2 *Jagdgeschwader* crossed the Ardennes front. A complete *Jagdgeschwader*, and a famous one rich in tradition at that, was doomed to defeat even before it ever reached the target. It was to prove of little avail that the *Jagdgeschwader* flew over 90 strong, or that I and III *Gruppen* were equipped with the Focke-Wulf FW190 D-9, some of them straight off the line and still short of their tactical markings.

Capt Hrdlicka complied with his orders, and it was only just before the operation began that he opened the sealed envelope he had received on the evening of December 23rd. It contained the operation instruction for Richthofen *Geschwader* which up to that moment had remained secret.

'Take-off 0800. Form up over mapsquare 'Papa-Oscar 4 and 5' and wait for II and III *Gruppen* to join. Target: St Trond airfield (Belgium). Attack to be carried out in conjunction with 4 Close Support *Geschwader* (Col Druschel).'

The inertia starters whirred softly. The mechanics stood back. The Jumo engines with all their 1,770hp sprang into life, to be throttled back and then run up. Soon the machines were rolling along the perimeter taxiway. In the grey half-light I *Gruppe* took off, throwing up clouds of snow from the runway behind them. The airfield was so large that the woods surrounding it caused them no problem. The 'long noses' took off southwards and straightaway turned west; to port the Grosser Feldberg fell away astern, and over Camberg the squadron set course for the designated assembly area over Coblenz.

From Nidda airfield, running from southwest to northeast along the stream of the same name, the Messerschmitts of II *Gruppe* under Capt Schröder were lifting off, while the rest of the *Jagdgeschwader* scrambled from Ettingshausen and Altenstadt. Between Giessen and Frankfurt the whole formation turned west to follow up I *Gruppe*. For 2 *Jagdgeschwader* Operation Baseplate had begun.

Ten minutes later the *Staffeln* of III *Gruppe*, flying from Wetzlar and Weilburg, reached the Westerwald—when suddenly black smoke began to pour from the engine cowling of Sgt Altpeter's D-9, blinding the pilot. Seconds later, almost before the others had had time to see what was happening, the engine was in flames. Everyone wanted to call him up and tell him to bale out, but that would have broken wireless silence. Sgt Fritz Altpeter of 11 *Staffel*, 2 *Jagdgsch-wader* did not bale out; he crashed to his death in his 'Yellow 4' near Dierdorf to become 2 *Jagdgeschwader* first casualty of the New Year. Having formed up over the Rhine-Moselle triangle, the formations spread well out and flew on west-northwest towards the High Eifel; from there they would head northwest to the line of the Meuse. Between Aachen and Liège they would be joined by the formation made up by 4 Close Support *Geschwader*, flying from the Cologne and Bonn fields under Col Alfred Druschel, holder of the Knight's Cross with Oakleaves and Swords.

Druschel took off from Cologne-Wahn with the Focke-Wulf F-8s*of III *Gruppe*, 4 Close Support *Geschwader*. Between Düren and Zülpich he set course for Aachen, the first German city to be captured by the Allies. Even before they joined up with the Richthofen *Geschwader* machines, the ground-attack aircraft came under fire from light and heavy AA. This claimed four of their pilots, One of these F-8s had Col Druschel in the seat. All that is known is that he was hit and must have come down somewhere south of Aachen. The fate of this *Geschwader* commander from Wiesbaden remains a mystery, and his name is still on the register of missing persons.

2 *Jagdgeschwader* also had a warm reception from Flak in the combat zone, and they too suffered casualties. 4 *Staffel* lost half its pilots that day.

Meanwhile the *Jagdgeschwader's* leading vics were approaching their target. St Trond was familiar ground to the Germans. During the past year II and IV *Gruppen*, 1 Night Fighter *Geschwader*, and I *Gruppe*, 3 Night Fighter *Gesch-wader*, had relieved each other on tours of duty there. As late as October 1944, the night-fighter ace Major Schnaufer, known to the British as the 'Spook of St Trond', was still operating from here with his IV *Gruppe*, 1 Night Fighter *Geschwader*, against incursions by RAF Bomber Command. The field itself, the hangars and the camouflage were just the same; only the occupants and the code number had changed—A-92 instead of 309. And now there stood on it, parked in long lines, the Thunderbolts of the 48th and 404th Fighter Groups, 9th US TAF.

As the German fighters went in low, the perimeter AA let everything loose at them. Pilots already airborne on operational sorties had warned the enemy by radio of the approach of a strong German fighter force. This sealed 2 *Jagdgeschwader's* fate. Almost every *Staffel* lost some aircraft, and the attack on St Trond was the last ever seen or heard of many a pilot. II *Gruppe* emerged relatively unscathed with two killed, but returned to base without its com-mander—a painful blow, as good COs had become something of a rarity in the fighter force.

But the German pilots were not altogether unsuccessful, even if the Ameri-can fighters they had set on fire and destroyed on the ground represented only a small proportion of St Trond's aircraft strength. Still before them lay the return flight, which took 2 *Jagdgeschwader* in a wide sweep to the north, re-crossing the German frontier near Venlo.

The machines turned back east, and 10 *Staffel* lost its sixth pilot. As January

* The Focke-Wulf FW190 F-8, like all F-Series marks, was drastically modified for the ground-attack role and was easily recognisable by its under-wing bombracks. (Author).

1st, 1945 drew to a close, one of the most experienced and successful *Geschwadern* in the whole German fighter force had received a mortal blow. The losses amounted to some 40% of the force committed to the operation—23 pilots killed or missing, ten taken prisoner and four wounded.

It was to be at least a fortnight before Richthofen *Geschwader* would again be in a position to mount a major defensive operation.

Success at Eindhoven

A lone FW190 A-9 stood on the tarmac at Störmede to carry Lt Col Bär, commander 3(Udet) *Jagdgeschwader*, to join his I *Gruppe* at Paderborn. Störmede was home ground to this battle-hardened commander for, before moving there from Erfurt-Bindersleben with Headquarters 3 *Geschwader* at the end of November 1944, he had had a previous tour at Störmede. It was from there that Bär, at the time with II *Gruppe*, 1 *Jagdgeschwader*, had flown on April 22nd 1944 to mark up his 200th kill by shooting down a Liberator. Since then the war in the air had exacted such a high toll in lives that the only way out was an operation designed to destroy a large proportion of the enemy's fighter forces on the ground and so weaken the German fighters' 'Public Enemy Number One'. That was why Lt Col Bär, like the other *Geschwadern* commanders, was about to go over the forthcoming mission with his *Gruppe* commanders so that they could then brief their *Gruppen*.

There had been a preliminary briefing on the afternoon or evening of December 31st, at which the *Jagdgeschwader* pilots had been told something of Operation Baseplate, although security had prevented them being told the details. At Paderborn 1st Lieut Seidel, the acting CO of I *Gruppe*, gave his 30 or so pilots a run-down on their mission. Capt Langer was doing the same for his III *Gruppe* and Lieut Müller, 16 *Staffel* leader and acting CO, for IV *Gruppe*, which had formerly been in the assault role.

In 3 *Jagdgeschwader* too, passes were withdrawn and alcohol forbidden as soon as the briefing ended, and the only thing left for the pilots to do was to go to bed. But on the airfields activity was intense. The army of ground crews worked without pause to get the slender Messerschmitts and the potent Focke-Wulfs ready for the morning's big show. On Luftflotte orders, the identification-friend-or-foe (IFF) set FuG 25 had to be stripped out of every aircraft on security grounds.

Reveillé sounded in pitch darkness. About 0700 there was a further briefing at which the pilots received their final orders. Only now were they handed the marked maps showing courses and fixes. And only now were they told the actual target: 'This is the airfield west of Eindhoven. It is swarming with Spitfires. So watch out for any Spitfires which may be already airborne and over the target zone!'

An hour later all was ready. At 0830 Lt Col Bär with *Geschwader* Headquarters and I *Gruppe* took off from Paderborn. At the same moment 15 Messerschmitts from 10, 11 and 12 *Staffeln* were airborne from Lippspringe; and at Gütersloh Lieut Müller roared down the runway with his Command vic, followed by six more formations from IV *Gruppe*. 'Assembly over mapsquare 'Kilo-Romeo two three, five and six' ran the order just before take-off. For as

N O R T H   S E A

AMSTERDAM

Rotterdam

G E R M A N Y

Eindhoven

R. Schelde

St. Trond

Dusseldorf

Cologne-Wahn
Cologne
Cologne-Ostheim SG 4
Aachen
Bonn-Hangela

Luttich

R. Moos

55-65
Fw190 F-8

R. Rhine

Ettingshausen
II/JG 2

Merzhauzen
I/JG 2
Nidda
II/JG 2

85-95
Bf109 G-14
Bf109 K-4
Fw190 A-8
Fw190 D-9

Altenstadt
III/JG 2

Frankfurt

PARIS

Mannheim

Metz

Karlsruhe

F R A N C E

0   50   100 Km.

ACTION JG2 + SG4 1.1.45

soon as the men mounted, total wireless silence was imposed.

The *Jagdgeschwader* formed up over Lippstadt and headed off west at tree-top height, the machines down to between 50 and 150 feet. They were on a set course and a Ju.88 pathfinder was to lead 3 *Jagdgeschwader* across the Rhine into Holland. Unaccustomed peace reigned in the fighters' narrow cockpits —no voices, no orders. The next aircraft in line still only showed up in silhouette, but it was good to see him there, for everyone felt this to be no mere run-of-the-mill operation. Even the old-and-bold among the pilots were feeling a bit of needle.

In well-spread out formation, with about 200 yards between *Stoffeln*, the machines flew over the north edge of the Ruhr, passed their first fix at Dorsten and crossed the Dutch frontier about 15 miles north of Venlo. Time to target about 20 minutes, and below them the flat plain of Brabant with the town of Helmond to the south. Over the Sonse Heath the formation turned south to make a wide sweep round Eindhoven and come in from the southwest over the airfield, which lay between the Eindhoven-Tilburg road and the village of Zeelst.

From maps captured by the British it seems that a small element of 3 *Geschwader* broke away from the main force before the attack and flew on west for a surprise attack on the field at Gilze-Rijen. Unfortunately it has not been established which sub-unit this was; and as some aircraft of 27 *Jagdgeschwader* were also targeted onto this strip, the aircraft reported by the British as destroyed cannot be identified. Perimeter AA alone shot down five aircraft, including an Me262, which may possibly have belonged to 51 *Kampfgeschwader* (Fighters) although no corresponding casualty report can be traced. The enemy suddenly realised that an unusually strong attack was coming in. In the AA positions the gun detachments doubled to their guns and tried to break up the German formations by intensive fire. 3 *Jagdgeschwader* lost a number of machines from Flak on the run in, some of their pilots being captured.

Meanwhile the Eindhoven field too had been alerted, but too late to take any really effective countermeasures. The RAF fighter units stationed there on January 1st, 1945 were:

137 (Typhoon) Squadron
168 (Typhoon) Squadron
181 (Typhoon) Squadron
182 (Typhoon) Squadron
247 (Typhoon) Squadron
400 (Spitfire) Squadron
414 (Spitfire) Squadron
430 (Spitfire) Squadron
438 (Typhoon) Squadron
439 (Typhoon) Squadron
440 (Typhoon) Squadron

Two Typhoon squadrons were already airborne, one on weather reconnaissance and the other on an armed reconnaissance patrol. Another formation was about to scramble, and Flight Lieutenant Gibbons' Typhoon

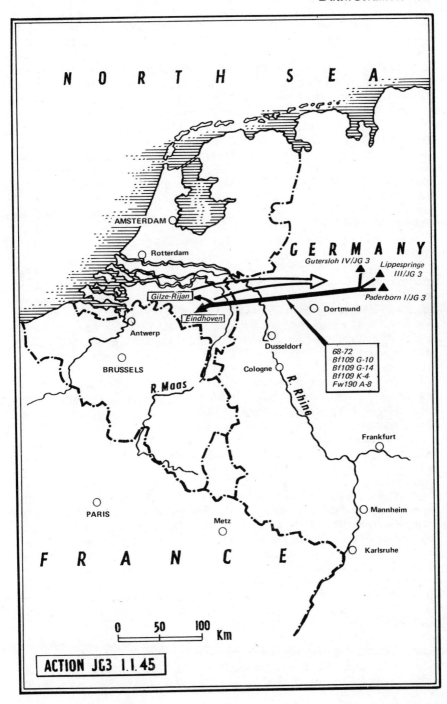

NORTH SEA

AMSTERDAM

Rotterdam

GERMANY

Gutersloh IV/JG 3

Lippespringe
III/JG 3

Paderborn I/JG 3

Gilze-Rijan

Dortmund

Eindhoven

Antwerp

Dusseldorf

BRUSSELS

R. Maas

Cologne

R. Rhine

68-72
Bf109 G-10
Bf109 G-14
Bf109 K-4
Fw190 A-8

Frankfurt

PARIS

Metz

Mannheim

Karlsruhe

F R A N C E

0   50   100   Km

ACTION JG3 1.1.45

was just lifting off as the attack went in. Gibbons managed to bag a Focke-Wulf before he was himself shot down, still over the airfield, by a vic of Me109s.

More enemy fighters tried to get clear. But they had about 50 German fighters over their heads, and the first pair of Typhoons, with Flight Lieutenant Wilson and Flight Sergeant Burrows in their seats, was shot down almost before it was airborne. The station must have been taken completely by surprise, but after the first few low-level runs the attacking aircraft came under well-aimed fire from the perimeter AA, making further formation runs impossible. Despite this the German pilots saw that they had gained surprise and made the most of it. The Typhoons and Spitfires, all drawn up in lines, made such a wonderful target that it was almost impossible to miss. As their machines swung in again, Lt Col Bär's A-9 set two Typhoons on fire, giving him his 204th kill. Fires were blazing all over the place. On a second run against some Mitchell bombers parked on the edge of the field, one of the I *Gruppe* pilots hit a refueller, which went up in an orange-coloured mushroom cloud.

The Spitfire squadrons suffered losses too. Five machines from 400 Squadron went up in flames, one of them from a German machine crashing into it, and four others were severely damaged. But it was the Typhoons which took the hardest knock. After the attack, 438 Squadron reported only two aircraft free of hits, while 440 Squadron only had two aircraft left at all, both of them severely damaged; and the four squadrons of 124 Wing could muster only 24 aircraft between them. Thus 2nd TAF lost a complete squadron's worth of Typhoons as well.

Meanwhile the enemy fighters which had already been on a sortie that morning were coming back in, and they joined the party without further ado. Squadron Leader Wonnacott spotted about 20 Messerschmitts pulling out of their run over Eindhoven and shot two of them down.

After an attack lasting more than 20 minutes, the last German machines turned away to the east. At Eindhoven they left behind a pile of ruins. Aircraft still burning, burnt-out vehicles of every kind, twisted sheet steel, and scrap-metal!

But the 3 *Jagdgeschwader* pilots now faced a long and dangerous flight home. To the west of Helmond 15 *Staffel* met four Typhoons of 439 Squadron returning from their weather reconnaissance, accompanied by two Spitfires. The resulting scrap lasted about five minutes and cost several Focke-Wulfs.

Battle damage or shortage of fuel prevented a number of machines from reaching their home base. Flak and dogfights had split up the formations badly; singly, in pairs or in small groups the pilots took the shortest route east. Although wireless silence was supposed to be maintained until landing, emergency calls or short messages were to be heard on air now and then.

All in all the attack on Eindhoven airfield must be reckoned as one of the most successful in the whole of Operation Baseplate, although it cost Udet *Jagdgeschwader* ten pilots killed or missing and six taken prisoner, a loss-rate of some 22%. At Eindhoven Allied 2nd TAF lost a complete Canadian Typhoon squadron, a substantial number of Spitfires and the lives of 25 pilots.

A Total Failure
At Babenhausen, II *Gruppe*, 4 *Jagdgeschwader's* base, the Baseplate briefing was held comparatively early. By 1800 on December 31st, Major Schröder had called his men together to go over the route for the next morning's mission with them. 1st Lieut Siller and a handful of pilots from his 6 *Staffel* came over by road from Darmstadt-Griesheim, where they had landed with I *Gruppe* after their previous sortie. Now the mystery of the Ju. 88 that had flown in to Babenhausen was resolved. The twin-engined night fighter ('What the hell's *he* doing here?', said a pilot) had been sitting on the field for several hours with the armoured Focke-Wulfs taking off and coming in past it. Its crew couldn't understand the strange markings on these aircraft, for the FW190 A-8s of this Squadron, formerly in the assault role, all wore the black-white-black band of Home Air Defence on their fuselages.

Headquarters and IV *Gruppe*, 4 *Jagdgeschwader*, with about 40 Messerschmitts, were based on the old Rhine-Main airship field; its giant hangars had been demolished at the beginning of the French campaign, to enlarge the field for military aircraft. On the morning of January 1st only half the Me109s were serviceable, although the groundstaff had been working on them all night. In dribs and drabs the pilots went over to the airfield from their billets in Sprendlingen to get their final orders from commander 4 *Jagdgeschwader*, Major Michalski. Studying the air photos at the briefing, the pilots saw a comparatively large airfield occupied by about 100 American Thunderbolts as well as some medium and heavy bombers. 'Mission—low-level attack on Le Culot airfield. The Wing is to form up over Bingen.'

Much the same was happening in Major Steinmann's I *Gruppe* at Darmstadt-Griesheim, which was to commit some ten machines to Baseplate. So 4 *Jagdgeschwader* stood ready for the attack on Le Culot—codeword 'Hermann'. For reasons which have never been fully explained, this operation was a total failure. As happened in 6 *Jagdgeschwader's* operation too, it can only have been a navigational error which left the target airfield, Le Culot, completely unscathed and put 4 *Jagdgeschwader's* machines into a completely different area. But that was still to come.

The controllers' flags dropped as dawn broke. The pathfinder aircraft was already airborne and had switched on its navigation lights to allow the fighter formations to home on it. About 0810 II *Gruppe* formed up over Babenhausen and hung around waiting for the Focke-Wulfs from 6 *Staffel*; but these were in fact already on the way with I *Gruppe* and did not join II *Gruppe* until Bingen.

From Bingen, 4 *Jagdgeschwader*, led by its commander, flew on over the Hunsrück, and in minutes or less they had reached the first fix marked on the pilots' maps, over Bullay on the Moselle. On they went towards Prüm in the Eifel, their second fix, reaching it at about 0840 just as the first rays of the sun lit up their machines.

From there they should have been over Le Culot in less than half-an-hour, but airfield Allied code number A89, north of Wavre and some 10 miles from Brussels, was never attacked on January 1st. What happened? We cannot ask the commander, Major Michalski, for he was killed in a motor accident just after the War. Neither his staff nor the pilots of the three *Gruppen* taking part

NORTH SEA

GERMANY

AMSTERDAM

Rotterdam

Eindhoven

Antwerp

R. Schelde

Melsbroek

Ophoven

BRUSSELS

St. Trond

Le Culot

Cologne

R. Rhine

R. Maas

Aachen

Koblenz

Frankfurt

Babenhausen

II/JG 4

Rhein Main

IV/JG 4

Darmstadt-Griesheim I/JG 4

50-55
Bf109 G-10
Bf109 G-14
Bf109 K-4
Fw190 A-8

PARIS

Mannheim

Metz

Karlsruhe

FRANCE

0   50   100 Km

ACTION JG4 1.1.45

can offer any explanation for the plan's having gone awry. But they were convinced they were over Le Culot. All airfields, especially enemy ones, look very alike in a snow-covered landscape. From its briefing on the air photos, 4 *Jagdgeschwader* was looking for a field full of Thunderbolts but Le Culot was not the only one used by this type of aircraft. US 9th TAF had P47 units stationed at St Trond and, in the northeast corner of Belgium, at Ophoven.

Several vics found no enemy aircraft at all and joined up with other fighter units, taking them for elements of their own units. The sky was full of German aircraft that morning. And so some alternative targets must have been taken on, wherever they may have lain. Some elements of 4 *Jagdgeschwader* which had completely lost contact went over to strafing troop concentrations on the roads round Bastogne—which of itself suffices to show how widely they had become scattered.

But once again it was Flak that was the Germans' main problem. And the enemy's shooting was good. Every *Gruppe* and every *Staffel* took losses. II *Gruppe*, or at least most of it, attacked an airfield that looked absolutely identical to St Culot, with the same mass of Thunderbolts that the air photos had showed. But this was in fact St Trond, Richthofen *Geschwader's* allotted target. The flak was already coming up and there was no time for a detailed check. Within seconds the fate of one Focke-Wulf had been sealed. 'White 11' with *Gefreiten* Walter Wagner in the seat took a hit that left the pilot no choice but to make a forced landing. In fact the damage was not severe, and Wagner had no difficulty in putting his machine down, which he did, just to be on the safe side, right in the middle of the enemy airfield. It was only when the Americans took him prisoner that he learnt that it wasn't Le Culot after all. But 404th Fighter Group got their hands on an almost intact FW190 A-8.

Other elements of IV *Gruppe* pressed on westwards and engaged an airfield that was also full of Thunderbolts with a few four-engined machines thrown in. 15 *Staffel* lost four Messerschmitts from flak.

The *Jagdgeschwader*, now completely split up and having failed utterly in its mission, turned for home. Whether 4 *Jagdgeschwader* had in the general confusion also attacked the Ophoven airfield has never been confirmed and remains a supposition. All that is clear is that elements of 4 *Jagdgeschwader* overflew southern Holland and lost at least five more pilots in the process.

In about four hours Operation Baseplate was over for 4 Wing. Only 30 remained of the 55 machines which had taken off. Seventeen pilots were killed or missing, and six fell into enemy hands. II *Gruppe* suffered worst, reporting fewer than ten Focke-Wulfs serviceable on the evening of January 1st; the former assault *Gruppe* was no more.

The Mission Against Volkel Miscarries

As late as mid-December 1944 Lt Col Johann Kogler was the only one in the whole of 6 *Jagdgeschwader* to know of the plan for a major *Luftwaffe* operation against the Allied fighter bases in the West. He had passed this information on to his *Gruppe* commanders at the appointed time, but neither they, nor for that matter II *Jagdkorps* or *Luftflotte* Headquarters West had been told at that stage the exact date on which the operation was to take place. Nor had targets and target data been issued. All that they knew was that it would be as soon as possible and that it would be launched in the early morning on a day when the weather conditions were suitable. Before the right day came the fighter force had been half bled to death supporting the Ardennes Offensive. The weather only cleared in the last days of the year, and on December 31st the operation order was issued. 6 *Jagdgeschwader's* target was Volkel in Holland.

The pilots were briefed by *Gruppe* and were thus able to familiarise themselves with the target airfield with the aid of a model. 'There's really nothing that can go wrong', thought Major Kühle, and he was quite happy about the way he had briefed his men in III *Gruppe*. Nothing left now except to make sure that his 'Gustavs' were correctly armed and fully fuelled.

The Ju88 that was to lead the *Jagdgeschwader* on the prescribed course into Holland and up to the southern tip of the Zuider See was already circling over Quakenbrück before the fighter formations were airborne. On the fields at Bissel, Delmenhorst, Quakenbrück and Vechta the controllers' torches were flashing clear for take-off. The first vic of 3 *Staffel* was just taxying, and Lieut Bauer in the *Staffel's* lead aircraft was already airborne, when 'Yellow 1' with 1st Lieut Pfleiderer in the seat suddenly lost speed and plunged from only a few feet up into the trees ringing the Delmenhorst airfield. The pilot was killed. The take-off of the other machines went ahead uninterrupted, but the first-lieutenant's death even before the operation was under way was a bad omen. 6 *Jagdgeschwader* was to lose ten of its officers that day, among them six COs or *Staffel* leaders—an unimaginable loss of command talent within a single *Geschwader*.

The formations assembled over Quakenbrück as planned and headed westward. II *Gruppe* under Capt Naumann was in the lead, followed by Major Kühle's III *Gruppe*, with Capt Trost's I *Gruppe* from Delmenhorst bringing up the rear—about 70 machines in all, flying at 500 feet. As they flew, the men were going over the whole plan in their heads, checking grid references and changes of heading and learning the compass bearings by heart. They knew that this mission was something special, for it was a long time since so large a force had been committed to a single operation. Every serviceable machine was airborne, but not every pilot had the requisite operational experience—something they were going to need in full measure before the day was out. Over Volkel, Major Kühle with III *Gruppe* was to fly top cover, while I *Gruppe* led the attack. Then Capt Naumann was to bring II *Gruppe* in from the south as a second wave and, when his Focke-Wulfs were clear, III *Gruppe* was to drop down for the *Geschwader's* third run over the airfield. Or that was the idea. But the *Geschwader* was still headed westwards for the Zuider See.

6 *Jagdgeschwader* had been formed in summer or autumn 1944 from 26 Heavy *Jagdgeschwader*, and a good number of the older, more experienced pursuit* fighter pilots were still flying with it. Among them was WO Karl Schubert

---

* The German 'Zerstörer'—concept had no exact equivalent on the Allied side, the nearest being the American 'pursuit fighter'. The aircraft mainly used were the Me110 and Me410. The concept called for a machine with a heavier payload than the normal day fighter, thus giving it greater range/longer time in the air and/or the ability to carry a heavy armament pack and/or armour. (Tr)

of I *Gruppe*, who recalls 6 *Jagdgeschwader's* second casualty on January 1st as follows: 'I was leading a vic, but I can't remember in which *Staffel* it was. After we got airborne from Delmenhorst we headed for the Zuider See. Right over its southern tip SWO Walter Jung went down. We assumed he must have collided with another machine. We never found out what happened to him—his machine probably caught fire when it crashed in a meadow beside the lake. After the operation was over I landed back at Twenthe with I *Gruppe*, 1 *Jagdgeschwader* and the enemy air activity was so intense I couldn't fly on to Delmenhorst till the evening.'

The night fighter allotted to 6 *Jagdgeschwader* as pathfinder was now over Spakenburg. The planned course ran south from here down to Veghel, then east and thence onto Volkel. But the pathfinder made a navigational error and flew straight on past the turning point, with the result that the whole *Geschwader* got much too far over to the west. No one can recall just who spotted the mistake first, but in any case only a few of 6 *Jagdgeschwader's* aircraft ever reached Volkel. Some others found themselves over Eindhoven in the curtain of flak put up to welcome Udet *Geschwader* but the bulk of the *Geschwader* went in on quite a different airfield, only about 10 miles northwest of Volkel on the s'Hertogenbosch-Njimegen road. This was Heesch, Allied code number B-88, and on it were stationed all five Spitfire squadrons of 126 Wing, 2nd TAF. At 0914, 401 Squadron's machines were out on the runway when the first Messerschmitts and Focke-Wulfs came roaring over the field at treetop height. Once again the surprise did not last long. The AA let loose with everything at the machines as they swooped down from all sides; the gunners had never seen so many German aircraft in the air at once.

A few moments later 401 Squadron scrambled right into the middle of the attack, shooting down five German machines—four Me109s and one FW190—of which Flight Lieutenant Cameron himself claimed three.

The bark of light AA, the rattle of machine-guns, the savage wail of engines on full boost and explosions on the ground provided the incidental music for the German low-level attack—punctuated by the thump of aircraft exploding on impact, for the attackers did not go unscathed.

When the attack went in on Heesch, two squadrons of Spitfires were already airborne on an operation, one in the Venlo area where it became involved in a scrap with a large force of Focke-Wulfs, and the other heading for Twenthe. The second of these, 411 Squadron, was just between the Maas and the Waal when the Germans attacked Heesch; it turned back straightaway and quickly made an interception, in which Flight Lieutenant Audet put paid to two Focke-Wulfs.

442 Squadron accounted for three Messerschmitts as it returned from its mission to find the party over its base in full swing. Flight Lieutenant Gordon was hit by his own flak and made a crash-landing in his Spitfire. British sources indicate that 126 Wing scored 24 confirmed kills on January 1st, for the loss of just one Spitfire.

Meanwhile it became clear that the German operation had completely miscarried. 6 *Jagdgeschwader's* sub-units had become badly split up and were now trying to concentrate again as best they could. They were flying hither and

NORTH SEA

62-74
Bf109 G-10
Bf109 G-14
Fw190 A-8
Fw190 A-10

Delmenhorst I/JG 6

Bissel II/JG6

Vechta

Quakenbruck II/JG 6

AMSTERDAM

The Hague

Rotterdam

Osnabruck

Heeschen

GERMANY

Volkel

Eindhoven

Antwerp

Dortmund

R. Schelde

Dusseldorf

Cologne

BRUSSELS

R. Maas

Luttich

R. Rhine

Frankfurt

PARIS

Mannheim

Karlsruhe

F R A N C E

0   50   100 Km.

ACTION JG6 1.1.45

thither over the flat countryside, diving onto various airfields under the impression that they had found the right target. Any semblance to a plan had gone by the board, and the allotted target, Volkel airfield, remained untouched. Stationed there were the lethal Tempests, two squadrons of which had just taken off on a surveillance patrol.* Three German machines, probably the only ones actually to reach Volkel, were reported shot down after a brief skirmish.

The rest were already on their way home. Some of them were chased by enemy fighters, but WO Schubert managed to shoot down one of these British machines, a Typhoon, to the north of Venlo. The *Jagdgeschwader*, now completely split up, headed east on a wide front. Its commander was not there, nor were two of the squadron COs. Only much later was it learnt that Lt Col Kogler and Capt Trost were in Allied hands; Major Helmut Kühle however was killed.

With Volkel completely unscathed and the scale of damage even at Heesch no more than light, the loss of a third of the aircraft sent in by 6 *Jagdgeschwader* seemed a very heavy price to pay. It remains a hypothetical question whether things would have turned out better if the wing had followed the correct, laid-down course. Maybe then Volkel would have been taken on, and maybe it would have been destroyed; on the other hand the Tempests might have taken an even heavier toll. In any event controversy continues to rage about the whole of this New Year's Day operation; but no blame can ever be laid at the door of the German fighter pilots.

The Tragedy Over Asch

At about the same time as *Gefreiten* Böhm and his friends in 9 *Staffel* were walking across to the briefing room at Gross Ostheim, Col John C. Meyer, at the Belgian airfield of Asch, had just been trying to get an operation ordered during the night cancelled. 352nd US Fighter Group, which had moved across from England to Field Y-29 (Asch) at the end of December, was tasked on January 1st for a wide-ranging fighter escort mission, accompanying strong bomber forces from US 8th Air Force to the Kassel and Coblenz-Trier areas. However Asch was so near to the line of contact that Meyer was unhappy about this and suggested that he should fly a patrol programme instead. Finally he got agreement to send up small patrols of Mustangs.

Col Meyer and his pilots were of course not to know that Asch airfield, about 10 miles north of the Albert Canal, was on the German fighters' target list for that day. No more could *Gefreiten* Böhm imagine that only an hour or so later he would be in a dogfight with this American officer; in fact he had never even heard of Asch airfield.

1st Lieut Fiedler, adjutant III *Gruppe*, 11 *Jagdgeschwader*, had first learnt of the major air operation just before the launching of the Ardennes offensive, when Capt von Fassong had held a secret briefing for his *Staffel*-leaders on the II *Jagdkorps* plan. Capt von Fassong, Knight's Cross, from Kassel, had been CO of III *Gruppe* since March 1944. For all the 100 or more kills to his credit,

---

* Among the Allied aircraft destroyed by the German fighter force on 1st January 1945 there was not a single Tempest. Even the two aircraft logged by Lt Col Bär as Tempests destroyed on the ground were in fact Typhoons. The Tempest and the Typhoon, both developed by Hawkers, differed in appearance only in the shape of their tail. (*Author*)

this was to be his last sortie; indeed the whole of his squadron was to suffer an appalling blood-letting, for just on half the pilots who took off never returned.

Meanwhile however, *Geschwader* Headquarters and the three *Gruppen* of 11 *Jagdgeschwader* were preparing for take-off. A Ju188 was already waiting at Gross Ostheim to lead the formation across the front line somewhere near Limbourg. On the other side of the hill, Colonel Meyer, with 12 Mustangs of 487th Squadron, was also getting ready for his mission. Meyer, one of the top American fighter aces, had decided to revisit old haunts and comb the St Vith area for enemy fighters. But things didn't work out quite that way.

1st Lieut Fiedler, who had been injured on December 23rd when he had to make a forced landing with engine trouble, had only rejoined his squadron on December 31st and was now to fly with them on this New Year's Day venture. A new machine, 'Yellow 9', stood waiting for him on the tarmac.

The whole of III *Gruppe* was airborne and had formed up by 0830, south of Aschaffenburg before Capt von Fassong turned in astern of the pathfinder aircraft and headed west. The Focke-Wulfs, flying low, were approaching Frankfurt on Main when the slim silhouettes of 25–30 Messerschmitts loomed up to starboard. That was II *Gruppe*, 11 *Jagdgeschwader*, from Zellhausen. And somewhere up ahead must be *Geschwader* Headquarters and the elements from I *Gruppe*. The whole formation was now headed by two Ju188s, and astern of them was Lt Col Günther Specht in his FW190 A-9. Specht, from Silesia, having started the War in pursuit fighters, had joined 11 *Jagdgeschwader* in 1943 and assumed command of it in April 1944; he now ranked as one of the most distinguished commanders in Home Air Defence.

The pilots had got over two thirds of their flight path behind them when flak started to come up . 11 *Jagdgeschwader* was now roughly over Aachen, in enemy-held territory. Suddenly 1st Lieut Fiedler's Focke-Wulf was hit, and the adjutant was struck on the head by splinters. He could feel consciousness slipping away; down and down he sank. He still has no idea how he managed a forced landing; nor can he recall foreign soldiers pulling him clear of the wreck and giving him first aid. He came round to find himself in British hands.

The German fighters flew north along the Meuse. They passed over Emael, then Kanne, Vroenhoven and Veldvezelt, names famous from May 1940. This was where the Luftwaffe had struck its first blows in the West; and was now about to deliver its last. 11 *Jagdgeschwader* was only a few minutes short of its target. The snow-covered heathland round Asch lay under heavy ground-mist, which somewhat impaired the visibility, but allowed the German machines' low-profile approach over fields and woods to remain undetected up to the last moment. The enemy on Y29 had no idea what was about to hit them.

Stationed at Asch at this time were four Spitfire units from 2nd TAF, 41, 130, 350 and 610 Squadrons, and with them 352nd US Fighter Group, mentioned above, from US 8th Air Force and 366th Fighter Group from 9th US TAF. One unit, 41 Squadron, was airborne on an armed reconnaissance over the Eifel at the time of the attack.

Led by Colonel Meyer in his 'Petie II', 12 Mustangs were taxying for take-off on the Belgian airfield. It was 0940 as the P-51 roared up the runway. Just before he lifted off, Meyer suddenly saw the puffs of Flak—and then he noticed a machine turning in on him, a Focke-Wulf flying low. Before the Americans realised what was going on, more fighters wearing the Black Cross appeared over the field. Meyer could not break-off his run and instinctively opened fire on the Germans as they closed him. But *Gefreiten* Böhm in his 'White 3' did not seem to notice the enemy fighters and held course for the twin-engined C-47 Skytrain* transports parked on the field. But the Browning bursts had struck home; in a flash the Focke-Wulf exploded on impact just by one of these transports, taking its brave pilot with it. Nothing like scoring a kill during take-off!

The airfield was now under running attack, but despite this the rest of the Mustangs, together with some Thunderbolts and the odd Spitfire from 610 Squadron managed to get off and give battle. The ground-mist had still not lifted and many pilots had difficulty in telling friend from foe. Flight Lieutenant Gaze in his Spitfire had just shot down a Focke-Wulf when he saw his squadron set upon by several Mustangs, who must have taken them for Messerschmitts. But no harm was done.

Now it was II *Gruppe's* Messerschmitts sweeping in, now the other two *Gruppen* Focke-Wulfs. 'All stations; target identified. Attack by vics.' Again and again 11 *Jagdgeschwader* machines shaped up for another run over Asch airfield. Parked aircraft, buildings and vehicles were hit. But the *Geschwader* paid a heavy price indeed for what later turned out to have been only slight damage. The operation had already cost six pilots.

Lieut Georg Füreder, whose 5 *Staffel* was the only sub-unit of II *Gruppe* to come through the day unscathed, gives the following account of the attack:

'After the briefing, held late in the evening of the day before, neither the pilots nor anyone else who had been present were allowed to leave the airfield. My *Staffel* was billeted in Klein-Krotzenburg. We took off later than planned because of mist-patches, and I think this did much to impair the success of the operation. The *Gruppe* took station in the *Geschwader* formation and set course for the target, following the two Ju188 pathfinders. We flew low, and the pathfinders relieved us of all navigational chores up to their breakaway point. This was the Meuse. One of the Ju188s behaved like any good bellwether and before breaking away turned his machine-guns on an enemy AA position on a bridge. He was a good shot.

'I didn't notice whether any of the aircraft in our formation were hit by our own or enemy flak on the way in, but I seem to remember someone coming up on the air saying they had been hit just before we got to the target. In front of the target we pulled up and fanned out to port and starboard; then we had a quick look at it and went in with our guns.

'I pulled up fairly straight and made my run almost without having to change heading. My approach angle was too steep for the Thunderbolts, most of which were parked on the eastern half of the field, so I drew a bead on four or five twin-engined machines over in the northwest corner and then pulled out in a tight 180° turn to take on the Thunderbolts on the east side. I pulled up level when a burst of tracer whistled round my ears. I thought at first it was flak coming up from astern, but then saw to my astonishment that I had two Thunderbolts sitting on my tail. One was letting me have it with all he'd got,

* RAF/UK name—'Dakota'.

NORTH SEA

GERMANY

AMSTERDAM

The Hague

Rotterdam

Antwerp

Dortmund

Dusseldorf

Cologne

Asch

BRUSSELS

Aachen

R. Maos

R. Rhine

Coblence

60-70
Bf109 G-14
Bf109 K-4
Bf109 A-8
Fw190 A-9

Frankfurt

Eellhausen
II/JG 11

D. Griesheim
I/JG 11

Gr. Ostheim
III/JG 11

PARIS

Mannheim

Karlsruhe

FRANCE

0   50   100 Km.

ACTION JG II 1.1.45

but for once his aim-off was too large. I pulled sharply up to port to evade and his fire passed astern of me. My pursuer and his wingman gave up, went into a powerdive and headed off west. I turned westwards too and to begin with I made to go after them, holding my height. But then I broke away and made a final run over the field, roughly southwards. At this instant I could see no more aircraft over or near to the airfield. The southern half of the field was covered in black smoke, pluming up from burning aircraft. I didn't try to see how many aircraft had been hit on the ground. I made my final run a bit higher because of the smoke, but still had to fly through the pall over the southern half of the field. But in all the hullabaloo not even the best of pilots could see for instance where the *Geschwader* commander had gone, and so on, once the first run was over.'

III *Gruppe* pilots were waiting for a signal to break off the attack. When they didn't have the enemy on their tails, they looked around for their CO's machine —and finally saw it away to the south of Asch in a dogfight with two Thunderbolts. Capt von Fassong has not been seen or heard of since. At this stage the men of 11 Wing did not yet know that they had lost their commander. Like that of nine other pilots, the fate of Lt Col Specht remains uncertain. III Squadron alone reported six pilots missing.

A bare three quarters of an hour after the attack had begun, the scream of engines and the rattle of machine-guns died away over Asch. The fighter formations, or rather what was left of them, headed for home. They flew north to begin with and then east across Belgium. But the enemy was still hot on their heels, and Col Meyer despatched yet another Focke-Wulf to chalk up his 24th kill.

In addition to damaging buildings of airfield Y29, 11 *Jagdgeschwader* destroyed seven British fighters from 350 Squadron on the ground and damaged three others from 130 Squadron. Several Dakotas were also destroyed. Four Mustangs of 352nd Fighter Group were shot down in dogfights, but all their pilots survived. But 11 *Jagdgeschwader* losses were substantially greater, amounting to almost 40% of the aircraft committed; and 12 of the pilots have still never been traced. On this occasion enemy claims and our own figures virtually matched. 352nd Fighter Group reported 23 kills on German fighters, the P47s put paid to four, and the British pilots one. This adds up to 28 machines out of the total reported lost by 11 *Jagdgeschwader*, which also of course included some shot down by enemy AA.

It was less than three hours later when the first machines came in to land at their bases east and south of Frankfurt. Many pilots only got back much later after having had to make an intermediate landing because of lack of fuel or battle damage. Almost every machine showed signs of hits.

When Major Jürgen Harder, a very experienced officer, handed over I *Gruppe*, 53 *Jagdgeschwader* and came to take over 11 *Jagdgeschwader*, he found very little left of this famous unit, which had played such an outstanding part in home air defence. And with the deaths of Lt Col Specht and Capt von Fassong, January 1st 1945 had cost the fighter force two more talented commanders.

26 Fighter Wing and the Brussels Airfields

Handrup airstrip, near Fürstenau, was a hive of activity—nothing unusual since Lt Col Priller had settled in there with Headquarters and I *Gruppe* of his 26 (Schlageter*) *Jagdgeschwader*. The 'long noses' were up almost every day fighting it out with the British, who were always on the prowl over North Germany shooting up railway engines, supply barges on the rivers and canals and Luftwaffe aircraft on the ground and in the air. Major Borris, commanding I *Gruppe*, 26 *Jagdgeschwader*, had lost 16 pilots since they had first landed at Fürstenau on November 24th, 1944.

The arrival of three Focke-Wulfs from Achmer on the afternoon of December 31st attracted little attention. This was WO Dietrich with two instructors from the special *Staffel* of 104 *Jagdgeschwader*, normally stationed at Fürth, near Nuremberg. Just as darkness fell a further 20 'Dora 9s' flew in—III *Gruppe*, 54 *Jagdgeschwader* from Varrelbusch. All these aircraft, were to join I *Gruppe*, 26 *Jagdgeschwader*, for Operation Baseplate. And they were scarcely on the ground when the briefings began.

Major Borris gave out the target to the 60 pilots; it was Grimbergen airfield, north of Brussels and just to the west of Vilvoorde. 'Operation maps will not be issued until tomorrow morning. Take-off 0815, when the two Junkers pathfinders are airborne. Form up over the field.'

By 0600 the pilots were on the field and picking up their map folders. The marked maps showed that the first leg of their flight was direct to Spakenburg at the south tip of the Zuider See. The second change of course was near Rotterdam, and from there the formation would turn south and head for the Schelde estuary.

It was 0814 and still half dark when the take-off signals flashed. The whole tactical group took off with Lt Col Priller at its head. Several engines were reluctant to start, and it took them almost twenty minutes to get airborne from Fürstenau. But finally all 67 Focke-Wulfs were away. As they were flying at only 150–500 feet, they had to make sure they kept a good interval between aircraft; and it was a well strung-out formation of fighters that headed for the Zuider See.

Between Utrecht and Rotterdam they suddenly found themselves in some vicious flak, which put paid to 2 *Staffel* leader, 1st Lieut Franz Kunz. The rest turned west of Rotterdam and flew on south. Once again they ran into flak and suffered losses. These losses naturally led to the German formation becoming rather split up. The pilots were getting angry because their own AA gunners down below showed no signs of stopping shooting. At about this stage the formation crossed the line of contact. Now they were over the Schelde estuary, and once again heavy flak came up at them. WO Steinkamp's machine was hit in the wing roots and engine. He tried to nurse it back to his own lines, but lost control and had to bale out into captivity.

Another to be taken prisoner by the British was Cpl Dieter Krägeloh of 3 *Staffel*, 26 *Jagdgeschwader*. This is his story:

'Our New Year's Eve party was cut short by a briefing. We went across to the

---

* *Albert Leo Schlageter* was a World War I officer who became a national hero when he was executed by the French in 1923 for his part in the resistance to occupation of the Ruhr. (Tr)

field early the next morning. My machine wouldn't start at first. Finally I got airborne and joined up with the nearest flight. We flew low. Some nightfighters guided us as far as Holland. Over the Schelde estuary we got above a British warship and caught our first packet. Two machines near me caught fire and ditched. My crate was still under control and didn't seem to be losing fuel, so I flew on. Then a bunch of Spitfires suddenly came up on our tail. My prop (a wooden one) was shot away; the engine over-revved and nearly shook itself off its mountings. So I feathered it and decided to try a forced landing. I was too low to bale out. Luckily I managed to put her down in a clearing in an orchard. I gather afterwards from some monks who pulled me clear that the wings were torn off and the engine had made an excellent bulldozer. When I was fit to be moved, I was taken to England.'

At about 0920 the machines were approaching Grimbergen airfield, clearly visible in the morning sunlight. The plan was to attack in three waves, but as the 50 or so 'long noses' came over the target about 650 feet up, the pilots saw that the field was empty. Just four Flying Fortresses, a twin-engined machine and a solitary Mustang stood parked between the hangars. The surprise the Germans had in store for the enemy had rebounded on them. Had our air reconnaissance let us down? The commander, Lt Col Priller, was understandably livid at such a strong force of fighters being tasked on to an unoccupied airfield.

So the pilots dived onto the hangars or the barrack-blocks, set the handful of aircraft on fire and destroyed a good number of trucks and refuellers. Suddenly there appeared on the middle of the field a FW190 on its belly; it was a D-9 from 104 *Jagdgeschwader*, and its pilot was taken prisoner. The Grimbergen perimeter AA had not yet been completely silenced and managed to knock down another of the attackers.

Lieut Nibel of 10 *Staffel*, 54 *Jagdgeschwader*, took on the parked twin-engined machine but came under fire from the light AA round the airfield and had to evade. As he was climbing, his engine cut. He dived to gain speed and tried to get clear of the field, but had to make a forced landing at Wemmel, northeast of Brussels, where he was picked up by Belgian police. Perhaps Nibel still doesn't know that the damage was done by a rifle-bullet in the radiator, which a Belgian resistance fighter had loosed off at him.

III *Gruppe*, 54 *Jagdgeschwader*, had suffered heavy losses the day before, and Operation Baseplate was a mortal blow for it. Of the 17 machines which took off only seven returned to base. Five pilots, were killed or missing; four were captured, and one was severely wounded. Major Borris' *Gruppe* had six killed or missing. 2 *Staffel* alone took five casualties.

As the last machine came in half-an-hour or so before midday, it became clear that the mission against Grimbergen had proved an expensive wild-goose chase.

All the better, then, that the rest of Schlageter *Jagdgeschwader* had a more fruitful day. II and III *Gruppen*, led by their respective COs, Major Hackl and Capt Krupinski and mustering 100–110 aircraft between them, were airborne at about the same time as I *Gruppe*. It was still dark when the pilots set off from Nordhorn for their airstrip some six miles away, on the Nordhorn Marshes between the Lingen road and the Ems-Vechte Canal. There II *Gruppe* Focke-

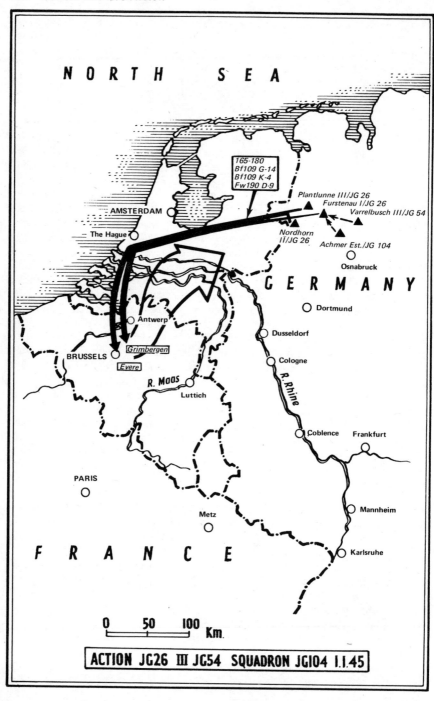

ACTION JG26 III JG54 SQUADRON JG104 1.1.45

Wulfs stood ready, and the snow-covered strip was lit up by the first rays of the sun as they took off to join up with III *Gruppe* Messerschmitts, flying from Plantlünne. The formations were led by two Ju88s, and their outward course was identical to I *Gruppe*, with the same fixes.

As they reached the Zuider See the air was suddenly full of brown-black puffs—German Flak! Two aircraft went down.

After changing course, west of Rotterdam, the German fighters flew low over the islands and causeways of the Maas and Schelde estuaries. Here the ships' AA exacted its toll, this time from 12 *Staffel*. They made for St Nicolas, leaving Antwerp and its harbour to port; soon the two *Gruppen* were over the northern edge of Brussels and a moment later Evère airfield came into view ahead. The pilots made out fighters parked in tight-packed rows and a large number of four-engined bombers. Quite a target! To improve manoeuvrability, the pilots dropped their jettison-tanks.

At about 0920, almost the exact time planned, the first vics swept over the airfield. At Evère surprise was complete. Three Spitfires of 403 Squadron had just lifted off, another vic was gathering speed, and still more were waiting to take off. While some of 26 *Geschwader* machines set about taking out the enemy ground defences, the rest went for the parked aircraft. At the same instant Sgt Burkhardt, 1st Lieut Glunz, Major Hackl and Lieut Sy each bagged one of the scrambling Spitfires.

Very soon fires were sending up thick pillars of black smoke into the clear skies over the airfield. Again and again the Germans went in. Refuellers exploded, hangars blazed, aircraft melted into glowing heaps of scrap-metal. The machines were parked too close, and the ravaging fire quickly spread; 416 Squadron, for instance, were left with only four serviceable aircraft.

26 *Jagdgeschwader* made between 10 and 15 low-level runs on Brussels-Evère before it broke off and set course for home just 45 minutes after the attack had begun. Their return route was the same as the outward course, but a few pilots finished up a long way off it.

The pall of black smoke over Brussels-Evère airfield was visible for miles, a testimony to the major success scored by 26 *Jagdgeschwader*. The *Geschwader* reported some 120 enemy aircraft destroyed, among them 60–65 fighters of various kinds and 32 heavy bombers—and this for a loss rate of around 19%. But even 26 Wing's success and its relatively 'light' casualties could not conceal the fact that all in all Operation Baseplate was a failure.

77 Jagdgeschwader's Last Major Operation in the West
From the outbreak of war onwards, in every theatre, 77 'Red Heart' *Geschwader* had always found itself in the thick of the fighting. It had begun in April 1940 when II *Gruppe*, 77 *Jagdgeschwader*, was the only fighter unit to take part in Operation 'Exercise Weser', the occupation of Denmark and Norway. Then came France and the Balkans, the southern sector of the Russian Front and later North Africa and Italy. When Müncheberg, who had commanded the *Geschwader* since October 1942, was killed in the Mediterranean theatre at the end of March 1943, Major Steinhoff took over. Under his command the unit took part in the bitter defensive fighting in Tunisia, and was later, together

with elements of 53 *Jagdgeschwader*, cut to pieces in the costly air battles over Sicily and the Italian peninsula. It was when it was transferred to Home Air Defence that the lack of aircrew reinforcements first began to show. The losses mounted steadily. In autumn 1944, 77 *Geschwader* was committed against the Allied airborne operation at Arnhem and had to pay a heavy price for its success. Between September 21st and 28th, 1944 it had 17 pilots killed or reported missing, among them Lieut Hans-Dieter Student, Colonel-General Student's son. A whole series of distinguished fighter pilots and commanders left their mark on the Wing—men like Bär, Deicke, Freytag, Gollob, Huy, Köhler, Leie, Mader, Müncheberg, Reinert, Setzt, Steinhoff, Ubben, and Wiese, to name but a few.

In mid-December 1944, when the launching of the Ardennes offensive brought about a sharp rise in fighter pilot casualties, the *Geschwader* took its full share. After particularly heavy losses over the Christmas period, little was left of the hard core from the Mediterranean days. Major Wiese having been very seriously wounded on Christmas Eve, Erich Leie took over on December 29th, and Capt Armin Köhler moved from 2 *Staffel* to take over III *Gruppe*. Now they faced a new operation. As the following account shows, it was to be a bungled one, not so much because of casualties, which in fact amounted to only 10% of those taking part, but rather because the execution of the attack went completely awry.

Before the German counter-thrust in the West 77 *Jagdgeschwader* was placed under command of II *Jagdkorps* and moved to its new bases in the Ruhr. I *Gruppe* was transferred from Schönwalde to Dortmund and II *Gruppe* to Bönninghardt, while III *Gruppe* switched from Seyring to Düsseldorf-Lohausen. On January 1st, 1945, the *Geschwader* was about 100 first-line aircraft strong. The groundstaff had gone to the most extraordinary lengths to get 100% serviceability. So this was a well-found unit, the more so when one considers that some fighter *Gruppen* were practically down to *Staffel* strength. But on this occasion a muster rarely attained by Home Air Defence wings was to prove of no avail. 77 *Geschwader's* punch was to land on thin air.

At Bönninghardt, Dortmund and Düsseldorf the preparations for Operation Baseplate by and large followed the same pattern as at other airfields. 77 *Geschwader's* target was the Belgian airfield at Antwerp-Deurne; and to get there the pilots had to follow a flight path of almost 200 miles. The direct route was shorter by half, but to ensure surprise the *Geschwader* was to make a wide sweep to the north, taking account of the configuration of the front line, and to fly into its target from Rotterdam.

Staffel after *Staffel* took off into the clear morning air. The machines at once turned north across the Lippe and in fifteen minutes they were over Borken. Visibility was excellent, and all was going according to plan. A quarter of an hour later the Messerschmitts turned southwest and headed for their third fix south of Rotterdam. As they approached the front line, the German Naval AA let fly at them with everything it had.

But the fighter formations had more than the German Flak to contend with. A mile or two from the east bank of the Ooster Schelde lay the airfield of Woendsrecht, also known as Bergen op Zoom. When several vics mistakenly

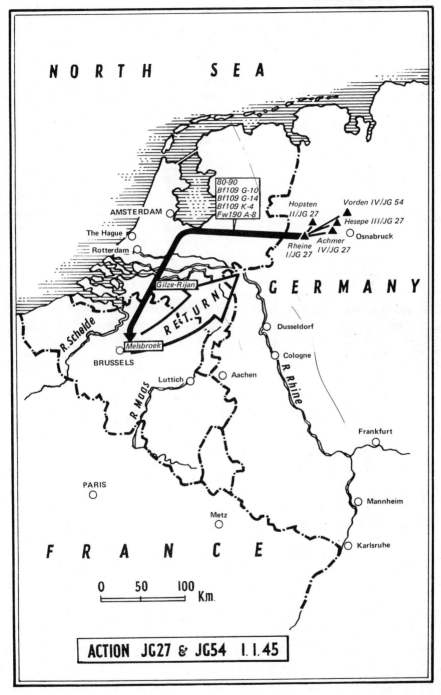

NORTH SEA

GERMANY

80-90
Bf109 G-10
Bf109 G-14
Bf109 K-4
Fw190 A-8

AMSTERDAM

The Hague

Rotterdam

Hopsten
II/JG 27

Vorden IV/JG 54

Hesepe III/JG 27

Osnabruck

Rheine
I/JG 27

Achmer
IV/JG 27

Gilze-Rijan

RETURN

Dusseldorf

Cologne

Melsbroek

BRUSSELS

R.Schelde

Luttich

Aachen

R. Rhine

R. Maas

PARIS

Frankfurt

Metz

Mannheim

FRANCE

Karlsruhe

0   50   100 Km.

ACTION JG27 & JG54 1.1.45

went in to strafe it, they could see hardly a single machine on the ground. The German pilots were not to know that all its five Spitfire squadrons were already airborne. Meanwhile the city and port of Antwerp, gleaming in the sunlight, loomed up to the south. Most conspicuous of all were the port, with the largest docks in Europe, and the towering cathedrals. But the pilots had little time to enjoy the sight, for as they crossed the Schelde up came the Flak. B70 (Deurne) was a base for British Hawker Typhoon fighters. Only one of them, a 266 Squadron machine, was lost in the attack, although another dozen or so were more or less severely damaged. Against this, two *Jagdgeschwader* pilots were shot down in the Antwerp area and taken prisoner.

The orders were that the pilots were to make four runs over the field, operating singly or in pairs. But it didn't work out this way, perhaps for two reasons —the unexpected diversion onto Woendsrecht ending in fiasco, and the strength of the British defences at Antwerp-Deurne. II *Gruppe*, 77 *Jagdgeschwader* appears to have been unable to find the target at all; the Messerschmitts made several circuits over the northeast of Antwerp, but they never attacked Deurne airfield.

After the failure of their attack, the *Geschwader* turned northeast for the return flight. They lost a further two aircraft on the way back, both from 10 *Staffel*.

Seen as a whole against an initial strength of some 35 aircraft per squadron, the losses—ten pilots in all—were very light, certainly in comparison to those of other *Geschwadern*. It seems as though one of the *Gruppen*, probably I *Gruppe*, shot its bolt at Woensdrecht and got completely split up. This means that only III *Gruppe* was over the target, as on their own admission II *Gruppe* had been unable to find Antwerp-Deurne. Thus it may well be true that only some 30 machines ever appeared over Deurne.

German casualty lists show four pilots as killed; and four were taken prisoner. The Allies, however, reported the capture of five pilots from 77 *Jagdgeschwader*. It may well be—and this applies to the other *Geschwadern* also —that the German casualty reports have some small gaps in them, in which case all the casualty figures given would tend to be on the low side.

The Losses

'New Year's Day 45—The Execution Order from the Bunker.'*—'304 Machines failed to return'—'59 *Geschwader* commander sacrificed to the murderous Allied air defence.'

How much truth is there in these headlines from the post-war press and other publications? Almost 28 years have passed since Baseplate was flown. Many of the pilots then reported missing in fact survived the war; as many again have had to be added to the list of those killed in action. Some four dozen cases are still open at the time of writing; of some of the missing no trace whatever has been found, so that no one knows whether they were killed or came back. But after over four years of intensive research the fighter force casualties on January 1st, 1945 are now reasonably firm. The resulting figures are published here for the first time.

* ie Hitler's underground command post in Berlin. (Tr)

AMSTERDAM

Rotterdam

Eindhoven

Antwerp

BRUSSELS

Luttich

Aachen

Dusseldorf

Cologne

R. Rhine

Koblenz

Frankfurt

PARIS

Mannheim

Kirrlach III/JG 53

Frescaty Metz

RETURN

Karlsruhe

Malmsheim
II/JG 53

45-55
Bf109 G-14
Bf109 K-4

St.-Echterdingen
IV/JG 53

R. Maas

N O R T H   S E A

G E R M A N Y

F R A N C E

0   50   100 Km

ACTION JG53 1.1.45

In Operation Baseplate the German day-fighter force alone lost 214 pilots. 151 were killed or reported missing (the cases of 48 of the missing still being under investigation); a further 63 were taken prisoner. In addition there were 18 wounded, but these cannot be counted as a total loss, since most of them were able to return to flying duties sooner or later.

While the casualties have now been established within a small margin of error, it is more difficult to arrive at figures for materiel; no list of aircraft losses as such is available, if indeed one ever existed. In every unit there must have been machines which crashed as a result of enemy action, German AA fire or technical failures while their pilots escaped unhurt. It is thus safe to assume that, in addition to the 232 incidents which caused casualties, a further 60 or 70 aircraft were lost, bringing the probable total for the German fighter force on January 1st, 1945 to around 300. This corresponds to a loss rate of 30% of all aircraft involved in the operation.

Enemy sources quote the discovery of 137 wrecked machines—98 in the British sector and 39 in the American; of these 57 are said to have been shot down by fighters and 80 by Allied AA defences. Adding to these the 48 as yet untraced and the 18 flown by pilots who were wounded, we get a total of some 200 aircraft. The rest must be laid at the door of our own AA gunners. These figures can in fact never be exact, as some of the machines hit by our own AA fire crashed in enemy territory and were thus counted in the figure of 137. Nevertheless the final total is probably not all that far out.

On the other hand the figure that is constantly being bandied around of 59 commanders lost in Baseplate is quite ridiculous. It is a mystery how anyone could ever have arrived at such a figure. The summary below shows clearly the actual number of commanders who became casualties:

2	*Geschwader* commanders (1)
6	*Gruppe* commanders
10	*Staffel* leaders (including 1 wounded)

18	unit/sub-unit commanders
+ 214	others (2) (including 17 wounded)

232 pilots
(1) plus Col Druschel of 3 Close Support *Geschwader*, = 3 in all.
(2) ie all ranks, other than those holding command appointments.

And while we are talking statistics, it is worth mentioning that 4 and 53 *Jagdgeschwadern* lost none of their commanders. As against this 6 *Geschwader* had the highest total—six in all. In terms of pilots, 77 *Jagdgeschwader* had the fewest casualties and 4 *Jagdgeschwader* the most. At *Gruppe* level, it was III *Gruppe* of 54 *Jagdgeschwader*, that suffered the highest casualties; of the 17 machines that took off only 7 returned—a loss rate of almost 60%.

Operation Baseplate amounted to a total defeat. The home air defence formations equipped with the standard types of fighter never recovered from the blow. Their subsequent operations were insignificant seen against the situation as a whole and offered no further threat to the domination of the enemy air forces.

N O R T H S E A

AMSTERDAM

Utrecht

The Hague

Rotterdam

100-110
Bf109 G-14
Bf109 K-4

G E R M A N Y

Dortmund I/JG 77

Bonninghardt II/JG 77

Lohausen III/JG 77

Deurne

Antwerp

R. Schelde

BRUSSELS

R. Maas

Cologne

R. Rhine

Frankfurt

PARIS

Mannheim

Metz

Karlsruhe

F R A N C E

0   50   100 Km

ACTION JG77 1.1.45

Controversy continues to rage over the entire operation. The gaining of a dubious advantage at the cost of 151 fighter pilots killed or missing, all within a period of 4 hours, can only be described as nonsensical. When the up-and-coming generation ask their inevitable questions, it will not be easy to make them see how all these things could have come about.

Unit†	Killed/Missing	PW	Wounded	Including commanders	Total Casualties	Av no of aircraft Committed	Casualties %
I./JG1	7	3			10		
II./JG1	10	1	1	2	12		
III./JG1	1	2			3		
	18	6	1	2	25	80	31
Stab/JG2		1			1		
I./JG2	10	5	1		16		
II./JG2	3	1	1	1	5		
III./JG2	10	3	2		15		
	23	10	4	1	37	90	31
I./JG3	3	5			8		
III./JG3	3		2	2	5		
IV./JG3	4	1			5		
	10	6	2	2	18	70	26
I./JG4	3				3		
II./JG4	8	3	1		12		
IV./JG4	5	3			8		
	16	6	1	2	23	55	42
Stab/JG6		1		1	1		
I./JG6	5	1		1	6		
II./JG6	6	1		1	7		
III./JG6	6	3		3	9		
	17	6		6	23	70	33

Unit					Total		
Stab/JG11	2				2		
I./JG11	3			1	3		
II./JG11	6	2			8		
III./JG11	10	2	2	1	12	65	38
JG11	**21**				**25**		
I./JG26	5	4	3	2	10	160	15
II./JG26	4	3	1	1	9		
III./JG26	3	4	1		5		
JG26	**12**				**24**		
I./JG27	6	8	4	1	7	85	18
II./JG27	1	1		1	2		
III./JG27	2	1			3		
IV./JG27	2	1		1	3		
JG27	**11**				**15**		
II./JG53	5	3	1	2	8	50	36
III./JG53	5	2	1		2	17	60
IV./JG53	2	2			8	25	12
JG53					**18**		
III./JG54	10	4	4	1	10	50	36
IV./JG54	5	4	1		3	17	60
JG54					**13**	25	12
I./JG77	7	5	1	1	13	105	10
II./JG77	2	1			3		
III./JG77	3	3		1	1		
JG77					**10**		
	6	4	18	18	10	875	
Total	**151**	**63**			**232**		

Unit†	Killed/Missing	PW	Wounded	Including commanders	Total Casualties	Av no of aircraft Committed	Casualties %
Est./JG104		1			1	3	
Stab/SG4	1			1	1		
III./SG4	2	1			3		
NSGr.20	3	1		1	4		
NJG1	9	2			11		
NJG3	3	1			4		
NJG101	1				1		
	14	3			16		
KG(J)51	2				2		
Day fighter force	151	63	18	18	232		
Other forces	19	4		1	23		
Total losses :	170	67	18	19	255		

In the designations below:-

Roman Numeral indicates *Gruppe* Stab = headquarters

Est. = Special *Staffel* JG = *Jagdgeschwader*

SG = Close Support *Geschwader* NSGr.20 = 20 Independent Night Close Support *Gruppe*

NJG = Night Fighter *Geschwader*

KG (J) 51 = 51 *Kampfgeschwader* (Fighters).

IV *A Forlorn Hope*

The Collapse of German Air Defence
Monday January 1st, 1945

As we have seen, Operation Baseplate broke the back of the corps of fighter pilots. But this was not the whole story. While the bulk of the fighter units were pouring out their blood in the Western theatre, operations over Germany itself continued.

To avoid leaving German territory completely defenceless in face of any major daylight incursions by Allied bombers, 300 and 301 *Jagdgeschwader* were held back at their stations in Central Germany. At this instant these two experienced formations constituted the entire home air defence force; normally their seven fighter *Gruppen* would have held between them over 300 first-line aircraft, by no means a negligible force. But now, at the turn of 1944/45, the earmarking of just two *Geschwader* to cover the whole of Germany was totally inadequate, for both were severely under-strength. Only the day before, on December 31st, both 300 and 301 *Geschwader* had been on operations, hunting the enemy down and worrying him like terriers; but that day too their recent losses had left their mark on operational capability. The enemy on the other hand was growing more powerful day by day. For all the courage and resolve they showed, the last-ditch deeds of individuals no longer cut much ice.

As the lead formations of American bomber forces some 1,000 strong approached the islands of East Friesland that January morning, 300 *Geschwader* was scrambled to intercept the stream of bombers, while 301 *Geschwader* was brought to cockpit readiness. I *Jagdkorps* Control Centre at Treuenbrietzen wanted to wait and see how things shaped before committing their final fighter reserves.

First contact with the US 8th Air Force Liberators and Flying Fortresses was made shortly before midday between Bremerhaven and Bremen. By this time the bulk of the fighters returning from their attack on the Allied infrastructure had already landed, but it was clearly out of the question to send them straight off again on air defence. So the Messerschmitts of II and IV *Gruppe* of 300 *Geschwader* were the only Luftwaffe units to take on the Americans as they flew in.

This time the Mustang escort did not entirely succeed in keeping the Germans off, and a large number of bombers was shot down. But as the battle went on our own losses also grew. By now I *Gruppe* had also arrived in the area of operations and had made an interception near Lüneburg.

South of Hamburg a formation of about 100 Flying Fortresses broke away from the main force and turned south. Its target was the hydrogenation plant at Dollbergen, about 20 miles east of Hanover on the Hanover-Wolfsburg railway line. They must have had a brief contact over the Uelzen-Soltau area with one or more Messerschmitt Me262s of III *Gruppe*, 7 *Jagdgeschwader*. This is evidenced by the loss of one of these jet fighters, when Lieut Lönnekker was shot down and killed southwest of Fassberg in a dogfight with the fighter escort. This aircraft must have been on a test flight or some kind of trial; certainly 7 *Jagdgeschwader* was not operational at this stage.

Meanwhile the main bomber force had reached the Elbe near Wittenberge. GOC I *Jagdkorps* now assumed a raid on Berlin and scrambled the whole of 301 *Jagdgeschwader*. The capital's air-raid sirens sounded at 1251 but the great city on the Spree was to be spared that day. The Americans changed heading in mapsquare 'Delta-Delta' and made a wide sweep to the south of Berlin, making for Eastern Germany. But first the heavy bombers came into the operational zone of 301 *Jagdgeschwader* with its three *Gruppe* of Focke-Wulfs, and bitter fighting developed south of Stendal. III *Gruppe* reported four pilots wounded near Stendal, among them Lieut Reinicke, 5 Flight leader.

To the north of Halle the Americans changed course again, this time to the west, and at last their intention became clear. The target was Kassel! But 300 and 301 *Jagdgeschwadern* had used up their flying time. Back at the bases the machines were refuelled and rearmed as quickly as possible and sent straight back into the air. But the German fighters could not catch up the heavy bomber formations, now on their way home, and had to return to base without intercepting.

On January 1st the Americans also bombed communications targets in the Coblenz-Trier area, and RAF Bomber Command put in an attack on the Dortmund-Ems Canal. Both these raids were unopposed; the two fighter *Geschwader* available in Germany had been drawn off by the operation against Kassel. They scored 16 kills for the loss of 27 of their own machines. 9 pilots, 6 of them from 300 *Geschwader*, were killed, 4 wounded and 1 reported missing over Central Germany.

The air operations of the first day of the fateful year of 1945 were over. Baseplate and the subsequent defensive operation were the beginning of the end.

Sunday January 14th 1945

When the crew of the Arado 96 TG + UK* saw a whole bunch of enemy aircraft on their tail, it was already too late. WO Hassinger and Sgt Foerster, both from 102 *Jagdgeschwader* reinforcement *Gruppe*, had taken off early on a training flight and headed south. It must have been about 1045 when the American Mustangs appeared; they shot down the lone Arado near Eggebek, killing both its crew. This marked the start of Black Sunday for I *Jagdkorps* home team, 300 and 301 *Jagdgeschwader*. These units had so far come off comparatively lightly, but now, two weeks after the sacrifice of the other fighter units in the

---

* This was the form of tactical sign used for all aircraft other than fighters and machines in the training organisation proper. Generally the two letters or letter and figure to the left of the Black Cross identified the wing by role and area, and those to the right the flight and the individual aircraft. (Tr)

West, it was their turn for blood-letting.

January 14th was a clear, cold winter's day. For the first time since the New Year US 8th Air Force was headed for the German heartland in strength. 600 heavy bombers in all—the Flying Fortresses of 3rd Air Division and some Liberators from 2nd Air Division—were already between the islands of Föhr and Pellworm and about to cross Schleswig-Holstein north of Husum, when the Mustangs of 357th Fighter Group, fanning out ahead of their bombers, chanced upon the German trainer at Eggebek.

Then the leading American formations turned southeast and headed for Schwerin on a broad front between Kiel and Neumünster. When the bombers reached mapsquare 'Charlie-Charlie' on their usual route in over Ludwigslust, the German air defence expected a daylight raid on the German capital.

But the American strategic air force, based in England, had quite other intentions. Their targets for the day were industrial installations in Central Germany, and in particular the large military fuel depot on the Elbe near Derben-Ferchland, some 8 miles west of Genthin. Other bomber elements were directed onto Magdeburg; and a second force about 400 heavy bombers strong was operating the same day in the Cologne area, attempting to take out the Rhine bridges there.

The Mustang formations screening 3rd Air Division had penetrated almost as deep as Perleberg when Col Dregne and his 357th Fighter Group met 300 and 301 *Jagdgeschwader*, which had been scrambled for an interception. A major, very costly battle was about to begin. Fighting was heaviest in the area between the Havel and the Elbe, and here the Germans took appalling casualties. The pilots made desperate efforts to break through to the bombers, but most of them simply did not have enough operational experience; their attacks tended to peter out and were not really pushed home.

Visibility was excellent and virtually no manoeuvre made by either side remained undetected by the other. But the Americans were quicker off the mark and continually got on the tails of the dapple-grey German machines; every attack on a Flying Fortress quickly turned into evasion of the Mustangs. At least five fighters were lost over Havelberg, and another dozen or more shot down in the Kyritz area. 13 *Staffel*, 300 *Jagdgeschwader*, suffered worst and was virtually wiped out.

301 *Jagdgeschwader* too, notably 2, 4 and 8 *Staffeln*, had heavy casualties in the same area. 2 *Staffel* reported three pilots having baled out near Kyritz, and 4 *Staffel* lost three and two other pilots wounded in the triangle Barenthin-Kyritz-Gumtow, an area of under 10 square miles.

The two German units fielded 189 aircraft in this operation, and in the face of casualties on this scale it is all the more remarkable that I *Jagdkorps* pilots succeeded in shooting down a number of bombers. Their most notable success was against a flight of 390th Bombardment Group which came down low to make its run onto the Derben fuel depot. By the end of a running fight all eight Flying Fortresses had been brought down.

The American escort pilots reported an encounter with several Me262s northwest of Berlin. These jets were from Capt Georg Eder's 9 *Staffel*, 7 *Jagdgeschwader*, based at Parchim. The Americans managed to shoot down one jet-fighter near Wittstock on the east edge of the Prignitz; its pilot was killed.

Meanwhile the main bomber force was over the area between Stendal/Tangermünde and Rathenow. Once again the German fighters went in, taking the Flying Fortresses with their bristling armament head-on, or diving on them singly, in pairs or in formation from behind, in the traditional manner. But only rarely did they succeed. The silvery Mustangs knew just how to protect their bombers and inflicted heavy casualties on the Germans.

The bombers had already been over their targets for some time, while a whole string of engagements was taking place east of the Elbe. At this stage the Americans finally sealed off access to the bombers. III *Gruppe*, 300 *Jagdgeschwader*, lost four pilots in the area of the lakes round Rathenow.

357th Fighter Group claimed 56 kills on January 14th; with it in the massacre over Brandenburg were 20th and 56th Fighter Groups, the latter being Colonel Schilling's Thunderbolt unit which had already made its mark at Christmastime 1944. One of the biggest dogfights of the day took place over the Stendal area, where elements of 300 *Jagdgeschwader* went into the attack yet again and lost a further five pilots.

And thus these two *Geschwader's* costly operation drew to its end. The following day's Supreme Headquarters communiqué put the German losses at 78 machines, while the casualty lists show 69 pilots, 39 of them from 300 and 301 *Jagdgeschwadern*. Compared with the number of sorties, this amounts to a loss rate of 41%. The enemy on the other hand reported many more kills—161 in fact. This probably refers to the total of aircraft kills for the day; taking Germany and the Western theatre together, the German fighter force lost at least 150 aircraft. Or perhaps that famous 'air gunners' multiplication table' was in operation.* If the Americans had really shot down 161 aircraft over Central Germany, 300 and 301 *Jagdgeschwader* would have had only 28 machines left.

Nonetheless our casualty figures must be regarded as very high, with III and IV *Gruppen* of 300 *Jagdgeschwader* (12 and 14 respectively) at the head of the table, 13 *Staffel* took a punishing blow with six pilots lost, three of them killed. But the hardest hit was 10 *Staffel*, with five killed. Then came 4, 6 and 8 *Staffel* of 301 *Jagdgeschwader*, with five pilots killed or wounded each.

The figures for kills on Allied aircraft over Germany are also conflicting. The communiqué mentioned above quotes 37, but the Americans reported only 9 bombers and 16 fighters (13 P51s and 3 P47s) lost.

Luftflotte Headquarters West also had a busy day on January 14th. As mentioned above, 400 US 8th Air Force bombers raided the Cologne area and a heavy bomber formation from RAF Bomber Command attacked the Dortmund-Ems canal. In addition 2nd TAF flew a large number of missions, mainly in west and northwest German airspace.

In the morning three Spitfire squadrons crossed the line of contact in the east of Holland on an offensive patrol in the Hengelo-Twenthe area. 401 and 442 Squadrons caught a number of I *Gruppe*, 1 *Jagdgeschwader* Focke-Wulfs forming up to take off and forced them to make a crash start. The British shot down

---

* The American four-engined bombers had an average of 6 machine-gun positions. If three or four of the gunners in the crew shot at an attacking fighter and saw him go down, each of them would claim a kill (which would probably be confirmed). Imagination boggles at the number of kills which had to be sorted out at the debriefing of a large bomber formation. (Author)

Fighter losses on January 14th, 1945

Units taking part	Killed/ Missing	Wounded	Total persc/as	Aircraft	Locality
I./JG1	10	1	11	FW190 A-8/A-9	Enschede, Twenthe, Venlo
I./JG2	3		3	FW190 D-9	Altenstadt,
III./JG2	1	1	2	FW190 D-9	Lich, Hagenau
			5		
III./JG3	1		1	Me109 K-4	Arnheim, Deelen
IV./JG3	4	4	8	FW190 A-8/A-9	Gutersloh, Lippstadt
			9		
I./JG4	1	2	3	Me109 G-14/K·4	Gimmeldingen
IV./JG4		1	1	Me109 G-10	Neustadt, Oppau
			4		
III./JG7	1		1	Me262 A-1	Wittstock
II./JG11	2	1	3	Me109 G-14	Gemmeldingen, Kaiserslautern
I./JG26	2	1	3	FW190 D-9	⎧Cologne-Bonn,
II./JG26	8	1	9	FW190 D-9	⎬Lengerich,
III./JG26	3		3	Me109 G-14/K-4	⎨Steinbeck,
			15		⎩Overath
I./JG27	1		1	Me109 G-14	Ibbenburen
II/.JG27	1		1	Me109 G-14	
			2		
IV./JG53	2	1	3	Me109 G-14	Bad Durrheim, Kandel
IV./JG54	8	2	10	FW190 A-8/A-9	Bramsche, Hesepe, Vorden
I./JG77	2		2	Me109 G-10/K-4	Dusseldorf,
II./JG77	3	2	5	Me109 G-10/G-14	Krefeld, Warendorf Zutphen
			7		
I./JG200	5	1	6	Me109 G-10/G-14	Brandenburg,
II./JG300	5	2	7	FW190 A-8	Havelberg,
III./JG300	11	1	12	Me109 G-10/G-14	Perleberg, Nauen,
IV./JG300	11	3	14	Me109 G-10	Salzwedel, Stendal
			39		
*Stab/JG301	1		1	FW190 D-9	Barenthin,
I./JG301	7	5	12	FW190 A-9/R 11	Haverberg,
II./JG301	10	1	11	FW190 A-9/D-9	Gumtow, Kyritz
III./JG301	4	2	6	FW190 A-8	Perleberg Pritzwalk
			30		
Total losses (Western theatre and Germany)	107	32	139	(incl 5 *Staffel* leaders killed. 3 *Staffel* leaders wounded)	

*Stab = headquarters

seven other Focke-Wulfs on take-off or over the Twenthe area. Meanwhile the third Spitfire unit, 411 Squadron, had despatched three German machines, so that the 11 kills claimed by the RAF tally exactly with the losses reported by 1 *Jagdgeschwader*. The British reported two Spitfires lost.

Over Münsterland another tragedy was enacted when IV *Gruppe*, 54 *Jagdgeschwader*, already much reduced in strength from the operations of the past few weeks, was set upon and cut to pieces by Allied fighters between the Dümmer See and the Mittelland Canal. IV *Gruppe*, finished up with eight pilots killed and 2 wounded. That made their flight on January 14th the *Gruppe's* last operation of the War.

Just before noon a group of Tempests from 3 and 486 Squadrons, based at Volkel, intercepted a formation from IV *Gruppe*, 3 *Jagdgeschwader*. In the dogfight which followed, Flying Officer Payton shot down and killed Sgt Helmut Kenne of 14 Flight near Gütersloh. On the same day IV *Gruppe* lost six other machines over Holland; four pilots baled out.

The general area of Kaiserslautern was another focus of action. Here a tactical group made up of five flights from 4 and 11 *Jagdgeschwader* and IV *Gruppe*, 53 *Jagdgeschwader* became involved with Allied fighters whose dual task was to cover the raid on Saarbrücken and to seal off the Lorraine combat zone. 4 *Jagdgeschwader* lost two flight leaders between the Rhine and the Haardt hills. Nearby at Gimmeldingen, the enemy fighters shot down two Messerschmitts.

Elements of IV *Gruppe*, 53 *Jagdgeschwader*, based at Stuttgart-Echterdingen, encountered some American fighter-bombers west of Karlsruhe. In the scrap that ensued Lieut Liebscher was killed and a second pilot was wounded and had to take to his parachute.

26 *Jagdgeschwader* was tasked onto the Ardennes sector on January 14th. About midday it met a strong force of enemy fighters over the Cologne-Bonn area. The outcome—ten pilots killed in action, three missing and two wounded.

At last Black Sunday was over; and the balance-sheet was a grim one. It bore witness to the German fighter pilots' desperate efforts to achieve something in face of all the odds by barring the enemy's way into German airspace. For the picture that the men in their Focke-Wulfs and Messerschmitts saw in their minds' eye was always the same—the daily destruction of German cities, buildings reduced to rubble, conflagrations and civilians dead and injured. January 14th, 1945 cost the German fighter force 107 pilots killed or missing and 32 wounded. The fighter pilots had shown themselves full of dash and ready to give their lives. But the air defence of Germany, and indeed German airpower in the West had taken yet another hard knock. The day-fighter force equipped with piston-engined aircraft was no longer in a position to make a significant impact on the course of events.

January 14th–17th, 1945

Night fighter operations in January 1945 remained far more profitable than the day fighters' actions. For the loss of 'only' 47 machines, I *Jagdgeschwader* night fighters could still claim 113 kills—admittedly not a very significant figure when seen against the number of enemy sorties. On the British side the trend was to make greater and greater use of the Mosquito bomber. These fast machines flew in almost nightly in an attempt to break civilian morale by harassing attacks on German cities. But they were seldom troubled by our defences; in the whole of the month only one Mosquito was shot down.

On the night of January 14th/15th a large-scale deception plan by RAF Bomber Command succeeded in diverting the defence from the real target, the Leuna hydrogenation plant. Nevertheless some of the 250 night fighters which had been scrambled in pursuit did find the enemy. This nocturnal encounter cost the British 12 bombers against six German machines.

Of over twenty night operations flown during the month, the largest took place on the night of January 16th/17th, when the RAF put in some 250 heavy bombers against Magdeburg. The city had been bombed by Americans during the day, and fires were still burning to guide the British onto their target. On this occasion only 128 of our night fighters were committed, and many of them were lost.

The Mutiny of the Aces

After the failure of Operation Baseplate and the cost of the January 14th air defence operation, and in face of the tremendous toll that these had taken of the fighter pilots, Hitler appeared no longer to give priority to countering the bombing raids on Germany. Towards the middle of the month an order went out from Luftwaffe High Command to air formation staffs transferring seven day-fighter squadrons to the Eastern Front, to support the Army in the 'struggle for freedom in the East'. The first to be affected by this order were 1, 3, 4, 11 and 77 *Jagdgeschwadern*, but the 'home team' wings were also to take part in the end-game.*

Conflicting orders, the disciplining of distinguished commanding officers and deprecation of the fighter pilots' personal achievements combined to bring to a head the loss of confidence in the Luftwaffe High Command that was once more making itself increasingly felt towards the end of 1944 and Operation Baseplate. Göring's standing among the first-line aircrew had long since sunk to nothing. The Commander-in-Chief of the Luftwaffe naturally did not remain unaware of this; back in the late autumn of 1944 he had called the *Geschwader* commanders to discuss what could be done to change the situation for the better. But so many differing views were put forward that nothing really came of this conference; certainly it did nothing to solve the crisis of confidence in the Luftwaffe.

General Galland's sudden dismissal from his appointment in the middle of January was the last straw. Embittered by the recent decisions, experienced, battle-proven *Geschwader* commanders, the senior fighter officers of regions, *Jagddivision* commanders and inspectors drew up a memorandum which put the situation as it really was to the Reichsmarschall in the plainest and frankest of terms, with complete disregard of possible consequences. Göring quickly made a day available.

So it was that about noon on Monday, January 22nd, at the Luftwaffe Club

* If this refers to 300 and 301 Fighter Wings, it appears that they in fact remained in the home air defence role. (Tr)

in Berlin, there opened the meeting that historians have since often named 'The Mutiny of the Aces'. But this name is scarcely to the point; there could be no question whatever of a 'mutiny', for it was not the interests of individual Luftwaffe officers that were at stake. The moving spirit behind this unique assembly was General Galland, seen by the High Command as one of those responsible for the failure of the fighter force and therefore removed from his appointment as Director of Fighters. Thus the reason which had brought distinguished, experienced fighting men like Graf, Lützow, Rödel, Steinhoff and Trautloft together on that January day was not simply to have a long overdue heart-to-heart talk with the Reichsmarschall. Over and above this, they were determined to subject the current Luftwaffe leadership to severe criticism, as set out point by point in the memorandum submitted by this group of senior officers.

A short extract from the draft of this memorandum will serve to indicate to the reader the problems which those taking part intended to have out with Göring. The reasons for the crisis were as follows:

'1 The dismissal of General Galland was incomprehensible to the men of the fighter units. He was recognised by the fighter arm as its outstanding personality and leader and—despite the demands he made on those under him—enjoyed its loyalty and love.

2 The frequent accusations of cowardice directed at the fighter men by the Reichsmarschall, and this despite the fact that their losses were probably higher than those of any arm of the Luftwaffe or the *Wehrmacht* as a whole.

3 Although he is held in personal and professional respect, General Peltz can never gain the confidence of the fighter arm, because:

  (a) At this turning-point in the nation's history he held IX Luftwaffe back from operations by imposing exaggerated training requirements, while at the same time committing the ill-trained day fighter pilots to battle with no thought for the consequences.*

  (b) He is not a fighter man.

  (c) He was responsible both for the operation of January 1st, 1945 and for the losses that followed the launching of the Ardennes Offensive (i.e. from December 17th 1944),† which together cost the Air Force:

    2 *Jagdgeschwader* commanders
    14 *Gruppe* commanders
    64 *Staffel* leaders.

In the view of the fighter arm these losses were basically attributable to command errors.'

Göring was accompanied by the Chief of Air Staff, General Koller, and a number of other officers. He was handed the memorandum, and his face hardened as he read it. Then Col Lützow, who had been nominated as spokesman, stood up and began to speak. This is roughly the course of the dialogue that ensued:-

'Reichsmarschall, Sir. In the name of the officers present I must ask you to

* This refers to the provision of Air support for the Ardennes offensive. (Tr)

† The offensive opened on December 16th, but almost all aircraft were grounded by bad weather for the first 24 hours. (Tr)

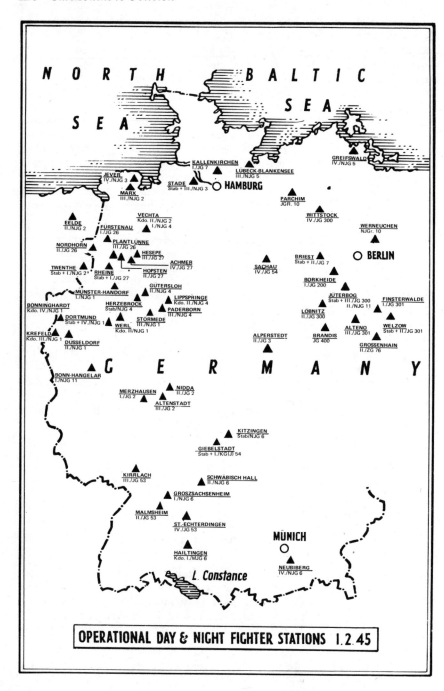

N O R T H

B A L T I C

S E A

S E A

GREIFSWALD
IV./NJG 5

KALLENKIRCHEN
I./JG 7

LUBECK-BLANKENSEE
III./NJG 5

JEVER
IV./NJG 3

STADE
Stab + III./NJG 3

○ **HAMBURG**

MARX
III./NJG 2

PARCHIM
JGR. 10

WITTSTOCK
IV./JG 300

WERNEUCHEN
NJGr. 10

EELDE
II./NJG 2

VECHTA
Kdo. II./NJG 2

FURSTENAU
I./JG 26

I./NJG 4

NORDHORN
II./JG 26

PLANTLUNNE
III./JG 26

HESEPE
IV./JG 27

ACHMER
IV./JG 27

BRIEST
Stab + II./JG 7

○ **BERLIN**

TWENTHE
Stab + I./NJG 2

RHEINE
Stab + I./JG 27

HOPSTEN
II./JG 27

SACHAU
IV./JG 54

GUTERSLOH
II./JG 4

MUNSTER-HANDORF
I./NJG 1

LIPPSPRINGE
Kdo. II./NJG 4

BORKHEIDE
I./JG 300

JUTERBOG
Stab + III./JG 300
II./NJG 11

FINSTERWALDE
I./JG 301

BONNINGHARDT
Kdo. IV./NJG 1

HERZEBROCK
Stab/NJG 4

PADERBORN
III./NJG 4

LOBNITZ
II./JG 300

DORTMUND
Stab + IV./NJG 1

WERL
Kdo. II./NJG 1

STORMEDE
III./NJG 1

ALTENO
III./JG 301

WELZOW
Stab + II./JG 301

KREFELD
Kdo. III./NJG 1

DUSSELDORF
I./NJG 1

ALPERSTEDT
II./JG 3

BRANDIS
JG 400

GROSSENHAIN
II./ZG 76

G E R M A N Y

BONN-HANGELAR
I./NJG 11

NIDDA
II./JG 2

MERZHAUSEN
I./JG 2

ALTENSTADT
III./JG 2

KITZINGEN
Stab/NJG 6

GIEBELSTADT
Stab + I./KG(J) 54

KIRRLACH
III./JG 53

SCHWABISCH HALL
II./NJG 6

GROSZSACHSENHEIM
I./NJG 6

MALMSHEIM
II./JG 53

ST.-ECHTERDINGEN
IV./JG 53

MÜNICH
○

HAILTINGEN
Kdo. I./MJG 6

NEUBIBERG
IV./NJG 6

L. Constance

OPERATIONAL DAY & NIGHT FIGHTER STATIONS 1.2.45

allow me to speak freely for 50 minutes and to give me your assurance that you will not interrupt. Unless you do this our aim, which is to put you fully in the picture, will be frustrated.'

'I've never heard anything like it!' Göring raged, 'Are you trying to accuse me of not having built up a strong Luftwaffe?'

The intrepid Lützow was not to be put off like that. He agreed that Göring had created a strong Luftwaffe and had used it with success in Poland and France. But then he told the Reichsmarschall straight to his face:-

'But since then, Reichsmarschall, from that moment on, you have been asleep.'

Göring was beside himself with rage.

'What's that you're saying?' he roared, 'This is a fine council of war! A ring of mutineers! I'll have the lot of you shot!'

With these words, face flushed with anger, he stormed out of the room. Lützow was relieved of his appointment and 'exiled' by the Reichsmarschall. He had to leave Germany forthwith and was posted as Commander of Fighters, Italy—an appointment which had long since lost any importance.

Trautloft too had to go and the end of January 1945 saw the German Air Force's last general post. Col Gollob took over at Kladow as Director of Fighters. Lt Col Dahl replaced him as Inspector of Day Fighters, handing over 300 *Jagdgeschwader* to Major Hackl, then commanding II *Gruppe*, 26 *Jagdgeschwader*, and widely recognised as an outstanding fighter man.

But the slaughter of fighter pilots went on.

January's End

After the transfer of a large number of fighter units to the Eastern Front in mid-January, only four day-fighter *Geschwadern* remained available to the Home Defence Forces and Luftflotte Headquarters West. And all four of them had been closed up and were well below strength. The Allied bombers in their hordes droned their way across Germany every day. The raids continued with unabated weight. Augsburg, Hamburg, Magdeburg, Paderborn, Bielefeld, Mannheim, Heilbronn, Duisburg, Düsseldorf, Cologne, Kassel, Hamm, Münster—these were just the main bomber targets for the second half of the month.

Our air defence in the I *Jagdgeschwader* area had by now become virtually meaningless. Our losses amounted to almost 30% of sorties flown, while our kills did not even amount to 0.2% of the enemy's.

In the last fortnight of January 1945 the fighter force lost at least a further 125 pilots, 80% of them flying close support on the Eastern Front. 7 *Staffel* leaders failed to return. 6 *Jagdgeschwader*, operating in the Oder-Vistula sector, was the hardest hit. It lost 18 killed or missing, among them two *Staffel* leaders.

On January 26th, the day that Lt Col Dahl was appointed Inspector of Day Fighters, I *Jagdkorps* was redesignated IX *Fliegerkorps* (Fighters).* The weak forces at its disposal from that point on left little scope for effective action. Only the formations which had converted to the new Me262 jet fighter were still to achieve successes which, though noteworthy, were in no way decisive.

* This was adding insult to injury. See sub-paragraph 3(a) of the fighter arm's memorandum.

Friday February 9th, 1945

The War had entered its final phase. To East and West alike the enemy already stood on German soil and was pressing forward relentlessly to deliver the final back-breaking blows. By now the Soviet armies had closed up to the Oder and were concentrating for their final major thrust on Berlin, while in the West the Allies were preparing their leap across the Rhine. Because of this, the enemy air effort continued to be mainly directed against communications targets and the fuel industry. But the Luftwaffe had little left to put up against the bombers' incursions.

Right at the beginning of February a number of German towns, among them Mannheim, Ludwigshafen and Bochum, had suffered massive terror raids. On February 3rd Berlin was subjected to a raid that proved to be the most damaging and the costliest in civilian casualties so far. Two days later Regensburg was the target for US 15th Air Force's heavy bombers. AA apart, our own air defence activity was slight; for the Luftwaffe High Command had issued orders to the wings that fighters should no longer be scrambled if the operation stood little chance of success. But the question was whether a promising opportunity of this kind would ever again present itself.

In the forenoon of February 9th almost 1,300 heavy bombers from US 8th Air Force, in several large formations, flew in over West Germany to take on communications targets in the German heartland. At the same time one of these groups was ordered to take out the hydrogenation plant at Lützkendorf, 10 miles west of Merseburg.

It was over the Rhine-Main area that the first encounter took place between the Americans and I *Gruppe* of the new 54 *Kampfgeschwader* (Fighters), which was ordered to intercept. 54 *Kampfgeschwader* had turned in its Ju 88s and, like 51 *Kampfgeschwader*, had converted onto the Me 262. The weather was bad when Lt Col Freiherr zu Eisenbach*, the unit's commander, led 15 machines off from Giebelstadt; as far as is known, this was the squadron's first operational mission. Near midday the Me262 jets sighted the bomber formations to the north of a line between Frankfurt on Main and Wiesbaden. But in breaking through the cloud the German formation had got so split up as to make a coherent attack impossible. The Americans' heavy defensive fire put down three German jet fighters one after the other. At noon the *Geschwader* commander was killed in action.

Some 70 fighters from 300 and 301 *Jagdgeschwader* were scrambled against the bomber formations heading for Thuringia and Saxony, but the chances of success appeared remote. Yet again, as on every occasion in the past, the Mustangs were able to screen their bombers effectively. For only two bomber kills the German units lost 11 machines, with four pilots killed and two wounded. There was no chance of warding off the raid on Magdeburg, for the American fighters had pushed forward in strength 30 miles or more to the east of the city and forced I and III *Gruppe* of 300 *Jagdgeschwader* to give battle.

Wednesday February 14th, 1945

The heaviest and cruellest air raid to which any German city was subjected in

---

* Freiherr is roughly the equivalent of baronet. (Tr)

the whole of World War II was only a few hours past. Dresden, the splendid Baroque city on the Elbe, had been obliterated. The folly of war reached its peak on the night of February 13th/14th, when the RAF, with a total of 770 Lancasters and a force of Mosquitos, carried out a two-phase attack on the capital of Saxony, dropping some 2,700 tons of bombs of all sizes. First estimates gave a figure of 20,000 killed. Home Air Defence could put up only 27 night fighters against this operation; their score was nil.

To complete the catastrophe, another heavy bomber force appeared over the Dresden area on the morning of February 14th. This time it was the Americans, who penetrated to Saxony via Kassel and the Harz Mountains—311 Flying Fortresses, with an escort of twice that number of Mustangs! Their bombs ravaged the already devastated city anew and sent another 10,000 to their death in the flames; for at this time Dresden was giving shelter to a host of refugees from the Eastern regions. At the same time two other terror raids were made—one on Chemnitz, and one, the seventh since the New Year, on Magdeburg.

On February 14th the Americans put 945 heavy bombers into the overcast skies of Central Germany. To counter the three enemy incursions Home Air Defence could muster only 145 machines from IX *Fliegerkorps* (Fighters); and once again it was 300 and 301 *Jagdgeschwader* who bore the brunt. On their own figures 20 of their aircraft went down. The Americans, on the other hand, lost only 2 bombers, a further testimony to the impotence of the German fighter force.

To the west of Riesa, in mapsquare 'Lima Golf 4', two squadrons of 300 *Jagdgeschwader* were in action against American escort fighters, who brought down a Messerschmitt from 4 *Staffel* and a FW190 from 6 *Staffel* in the Oschatz area.

Meanwhile III *Gruppe* Messerschmitts had scrambled from Jüterbog and reached the operational zone. They intercepted just after crossing the Elbe, and this encounter cost the lives of two pilots. Unhampered and in drill formation the American bombers flew on toward their targets. Fighter-bomber formations went over to low-level attacks, turning their guns on anything left over from the bombing. And the home air defence fighter units were impotent; they could do nothing more to put up an effective defence against the resulting inferno.

301 *Jagdgeschwader*, in particular the elements of II *Gruppe* from Welzow, had its losses too. 1 *Jagddivision* ended the day with ten pilots killed and 1 wounded.

And after the Americans had reduced three cities of Central Germany to rubble and twisted metal overhung with the stench of death, the late afternoon of February 14th brought action for Luftflotte Headquarters West in the shape of an encounter between British Spitfire formations and the Focke-Wulfs of III *Gruppe*, 54 *Jagdgeschwader*,* which was flying take-off and landing cover over the Rheine fields for the Me 262 jets of 51 *Kampfgeschwader* (Fighters).

In 2 TAF's favourite hunting-ground, the Rheine-Osnabrück area, Sgt Sei-

---

* III *Gruppe*, 54 *Jagdgeschwader*, had been withdrawn from the Russian Front in summer '43 and placed under command 26 *Jagdgeschwader* in the West. With effect from February 25th, 1945 the *Gruppe* was absorbed by 26 *Jagdgeschwader* and redesignated IV *Gruppe*. (Author).

denfuss and Cpl Zogbaum fell to the guns of Flight-Sergeant Moyle and Flight Lieutenant Woolley of 41 Squadron (Spitfires). Shortly after 1700 Flight Lieutenant Gaze of 610 Squadron despatched a Me262 with WO Hofmann in the seat; the machine crashed near Emmerich, killing the pilot.

German night fighters were to score one more major success before the war ended. A massive terror raid on Dortmund on the night of February 20th/21st had cost the British 25 heavy bombers. The following night, in a two-wave attack on Duisburg and a raid on Worms, 62 more British bombers were shot down. On the evening of Wednesday February 21st over 800 enemy four-engined machines flew in over Germany, 450 of them headed for Duisburg. 129 night fighters from 1, 2, 3, 4 and 6 Night Fighter *Geschwadern* were scrambled against this RAF Bomber Command operation.

In the moonlit skies bitter fighting developed and spread out over wide areas. Of the 62 kills, 28 or 45% were added to the tallies of just four night fighter pilots, SWO Bahr of 6 *Geschwader* shot seven bombers down; and Capt Hager of II *Gruppe*, 1 *Geschwader*, knocked eight out of the sky within the space of 17 minutes. Capt Rökker, leader of 2 *Staffel*, 2 *Geschwader*, sent six heavy bombers down, and Major Schnaufer, commander 4 *Geschwader* and undoubtedly the greatest German night fighter ace, accounted for seven.

Over the whole of the Ruhr, the Me110s, Ju88s and He219s worried away at the enemy. The ground control centres directed their pilots on to the bomber formations passing to and fro, and pilots then sought out their targets. Dark tracer* criss-crossed the shining white identification stars of the British aircraft, and gaudy torches of flame, plunging like comets, marked the end of the bombers. Traffic was brisk on all the night fighter nets.

It was the Mosquito long-range night fighters, whose task was to escort and protect the bombers, that posed the greatest threat and brought about most of the German losses. South of Duisburg, Capt Schirmacher and WO Waldmann, the crew of Heinkel 219 'G9+TH' from 1 *Staffel*, 1 *Geschwader*, had to make a forced landing in which Waldmann, the operator, was injured. A Me110 from 9 *Staffel* of the same wing was shot down by a Mosquito night-fighter $1\frac{1}{2}$ miles east of Störmede.

On the night of February 21st/22nd, the British lost about 8% of the bombers committed against Duisburg and Worms. But what makes the measure of success even more remarkable is our own very light losses of only four aircraft. Six aircrew were killed and two wounded.

While the major air battle was in progress over the West and Southwest, the RAF also flew about 100 Mosquito bomber sorties in two groups for a harassing raid on Berlin. For the first time the Me262 B-la/U1, a night-fighter version with the 'Lichtenstein' SN-2 electronic system, went up to meet them. These machines, from 10 *Staffel*, 11 Night Fighter *Geschwader*, under 1st Lieut Welter ('Welter Force') were based at Jüterbog; they had specialised in Mosquito interception, as the Me262 had the performance to hold these fast, highly manoeuvrable British bombers. That night they shot down three Mosquitos over Berlin.

* A special type of tracer for use at night, giving a visible glow but not bright enough to impair night adaptation. (Tr)

But in proportion to the RAF Bomber Command effort, the British casualties in those February nights were light, only exceeding those of the previous month by rather under 2%.*

Sunday February 25th, 1945
The closing days of February were marked by another period of unusually intensive enemy air activity over Germany. On February 24th strong US 8th Air Force heavy bomber formations attacked hydrogenation plants in the Hamburg and Hanover areas. These raids met no opposition and only two bombers failed to return.

On the following day the Americans launched a major operation against the German communications system, at the same time attacking a number of airfields, mainly those used by Me262 units. The towns of Aschaffenburg, Friedrichshafen, Munich and Ulm also suffered raids of varying weight. The American fighter escort, over 600 strong, once again succeeded in holding off the German fighter defence and allowing the 1,177 heavy bombers used to reach their targets unimpeded. The RAF also flew another daylight operation, this time against Dortmund.

IX *Fliegerkorps* (Fighters) scrambled a large number of fighter units against this massive incursion, but all were immediately contained by the escort fighters or the Allied fighter-bombers, which were out in strength. Elements of I *Gruppe*, 2 (Richthofen) *Jagdgeschwader*, took off from the strip at Merzhausen in the Taunus Hills to intercept a Liberator formation returning from a raid on Aschaffenburg. A spectacular dogfight between the units Focke-Wulfs and the American escort fighters developed over Gross Umstadt. A group of twelve Mustangs and six Lightnings dived on the handful of German machines and shot two down.

27 *Jagdgeschwader* once again took substantial casualties when its four squadrons became involved with British fighters over the Münster-Osnabrück area. 1, 2 and 3 *Staffeln* lost one pilot each. The whole Münster Basin was suddenly alive with enemy aircraft, and one German machine after another went down in face of these crushing odds.

In the same area I and II *Gruppen*, 26 *Jagdgeschwader*, reported contact. Both squadrons were flying FW190 D-9s, and Flight Lieutenant Reid of 41 Squadron shot one of these machines down between Gronau and Rheine—very probably that of 1st Lieut Kittelmann, who failed to return from this operation. Born in 1914, Kittelmann was one of the old and bold among the fighter pilots; he flew with 2 *Staffel*, which had two other pilots killed that day.

5 *Staffel* was just taking off from Nordhorn when some Tempests bounced the airfield and shot up the 'long noses', wounding Lieut Bott. Other elements of the two 26 *Jagdgeschwader Gruppen* were directed onto the Cologne area, where they encountered a Thunderbolt formation and lost two aircraft.

A Mustang pilot from US 364th Fighter Group had a rare bit of luck when he caught a twin-jet Arado 234 B from 76 *Kampfgeschwader* (Fighters) over Bohmte, about 10 miles south of the Dümmer See, and shot it down, killing the

---

* It is not clear whether the 2% increase refers to British losses (as translated) or to German night fighter losses. *Ed note*

pilot, Sgt Przetak. And in an attack on Giebelstadt airfield US 55th Fighter Group destroyed a total of 6 Me262s from II *Gruppe*, 54 *Kampfgeschwader* (Fighters), which were on a training flight. Three of these pilots were killed. In the Nuremberg area the Mustangs spotted two Messerschmitt G-14s belonging to 104th Fighter Wing at Roth, and shot them down in quick succession.

Apart from three flights of 301 *Jagdgeschwader*, the IX *Fliegerkorps* (Fighters) units scrambled against US 8th Air Force had no contact. The American force attacking communications centres in 1 *Jagddivision* sector had railway junctions in the triangle Salzwedel-Stendal-Wittenberge on their target list. Over mapsquare 'Echo Charlie 4' 1 *Staffel*, 301 *Jagdgeschwader*, led by Lieut Benning, an old hand from the single-seater night fighter days with over 20 kills to his name, became involved with the enemy fighter escort over Salzwedel. This encounter cost the *Staffel* three Focke-Wulfs and the lives of their pilots.

V *The Hunt is Up*

Friday March 2nd, 1945

Not the least of the indications that the Allies now sought to put a speedy end to the War was the further intensification of their air activity. On no single day or night of the month of March did German airspace remain free of their intrusions; and only a few weeks before the end of the murderous worldwide conflagration many more cities had to suffer further heavy air-raids with appalling results; among them were Berlin, Dortmund, Chemnitz, Dessau, Essen, Hanau, Hildesheim, Mannheim, Paderborn, Ulm, Unna and Würzburg.

The German air defence had been shattered. The *Geschwadern*, most of them by now reduced almost to *Gruppe* strength, went down in a series of last desperate encounters. March 2nd was to spell the end for 301 *Jagdgeschwader Gruppen*, but first a number of skirmishes in the familiar battleground of Rheine-Osnabrück provided a curtain-raiser for the major air battles.

It was still early morning when two squadrons each of Tempests and Spitfires from 2nd TAF took off on one of their surveillance patrols over the Me262 airfields. These had become almost a daily routine, for the Allies never gave the German jet-fighter units a moment's peace. And almost every day they led to encounters with German fighters trying to keep the British away from these fields or at least to prevent the jets being attacked during take-off and landing, when they were at their most vulnerable. That Friday it was the turn of some Focke-Wulfs from II *Gruppe*, 26 *Jagdgeschwader*, and a stronger force of Messerschmitts of II, III and IV *Gruppen*, 27 *Jagdgeschwader*.

The German machines had been airborne only a few minutes when a dogfight started between the Tempests and 27 *Geschwader* K-4s in the Osnabrück area. And when the Spitfires joined in the German pilots had their work cut out to avoid being completely wiped out. 27 *Geschwader* lost four pilots over the western spurs of the Teutoburger Wald.

After this encounter the British claimed a total of eight Messerschmitts shot down, one of them by Wing Commander Keefer, and two Focke-Wulfs. The German fighters accounted for two Spitfires.

As the morning wore on strong American bomber formations, with an overwhelming fighter escort, penetrated as far as the Elbe and flew on into Saxony. Some 200 German home air defence fighters were scrambled against them, and intense fighting developed at various places, stretching in some cases as far south as Sudetenland.

One of the centres of this fighting was over the south edge of Annaburg Heath between the Elbe and the Black Elster. In this encounter with the Americans II (Assault) *Gruppe*, 300 *Jagdgeschwader*, lost four pilots. III Squadron intercepted about 17 miles from its base at Jüterbog, in mapsquare 'Hotel Foxtrot', and lost two pilots in the Belzig area.

Another focus formed north of Magdeburg. 301 *Jagdgeschwader* had once again put every serviceable machine into the air against US 8th Air Force's heavy bomber formations. Its newly-formed IV *Gruppe* took off on its first and last operation. The unit succeeded in shooting down a few bombers, but the Mustangs quickly gained the upper hand and the battle ended in defeat for 301 *Jagdgeschwader*. By the time they landed back at their bases—Finsterwalde, Gahro, Gardelegen, Stendal and Welzow—17 pilots had been killed or reported missing.

Fighter losses on March 2nd, 1945

Units taking part	Killed/ missing	Wounded	Total pers/cas	Aircraft	Locality
I./JG2	3	2	5	FW190 D-9	Mainz area
III./JG26	1		1	FW190 D-9	Osnabruck, Rheine
II./JG27	1		1	Me109 G-14	Achmer, Saerbeck
III./JG27	3		3	Me109 K-4	Steinbeck,
IV./JG27	2	2	4	Me109 K-4	Tecklenburg
			8		
II./JG300	4		4	FW190 A-8	Belzig, Gross-
III./JG300	2	1	3	Me109 G-10	treben, Torgau, Saxony area
			7		
I./JG301	3		3	FW190 A-8/A-9	Aussig, Burg,
II./JG301	6	1	7	FW190 A-9/D-9	Dresden, Stresow,
IV./JG301	8	5	13	Me109 G-10	Wurschwitz
			23		
Total losses	33	11	44	(incl 1 *Gruppe* commander and 2 *Staffel* leaders killed)	
(against incursions from West and South)					

IV *Gruppe*, 301 *Jagdgeschwader*, met its fate some 25 miles southeast of its base at Gardelegen, when its three *Staffeln* tried to head off the American bomber force directed onto Magdeburg. The enemy fighter escort was too strong for the Germans; between Magdeburg and Burg a veritable massacre ensued, some 20 Messerschmitts being shot out of the sky in quick succession. The fighting over mapsquares 'Golf Delta' and 'Hotel Delta' became one vast dogfight. The brave young German pilots made desperate efforts to limit the scale of the disaster; and a few of them did succeed in bringing fire to bear on the silver Mustangs, so that they should at least go down fighting.

With four pilots killed and two wounded, 13 *Staffel* too suffered severely, the more so as the flight leader, 1st Lieut Johann Patek, was amongst the dead.

Away to the south, over southern Saxony and the Moravian marshes, the Americans took on the bulk of II *Gruppe*, 301 *Jagdgeschwader*. Here it was 8 *Staffel* that took the worst punishment; their encounter with the Mustangs cost them three pilots killed and one wounded. The flight had just received its first Focke-Wulf 190 D-9s, replacing the A-9 version.

For the IX *Fliegerkorps* (Fighters) units the day of March 2nd ended with a loss of 43 aircraft against 15 kills. 300 and 301 *Jagdgeschwader* together had 23 pilots killed and one reported missing.

But that was not the end of the story. In the afternoon a fairly strong formation of Martin B26 Marauder twin-engined bombers from 9th US TAF was targetted onto a military depot near Giessen. As the Americans approached the Rhine-Main sector I *Gruppe*, 2 *Jagdgeschwader*, which was to lose its commander, Capt Hrdlicka over the Vogelsberg on March 25th, was scrambled. The Germans intercepted near Mainz, and the normal dogfights with the fighter escort quickly developed. By then it was around 1730. The Focke-Wulf pilots tried running in on the B26s from every imaginable angle, but could not get into a firing position. Only one Marauder went down, and three German pilots were killed.

March 18th–19th, 1945

Search-and-destroy sorties against the enemy fighter-bombers and other ground-attack aircraft continued, but defence against the heavy bomber formations made little further impact. The jet-fighter units, on the other hand, were rather more successful, even though enemy domination of German airspace and the effects of raids on fuel installations meant that they could only be used intermittently. Mention must be made at this point of General Galland's '44 Fighter Force' with its Me262s; Galland himself has given a full account of its setting up and operation.* This force was made up of experienced and highly decorated fighter pilots; operating in conjunction with LtCol. Bär's 2 Fighter Reinforcement *Geschwader*, it was to have further successes against the American bomber forces. But to pose a real threat to the Allies, a far stronger jet-fighter force would have been needed. Plans along these lines did indeed exist, but the tumultuous course of events prevented their ever reaching fruition.

On March 18th a force of over 1,200 heavy bombers, bombing through heavy cloud cover, delivered another shattering blow on Berlin. Some 40 Me262s, including Major Sinner's III *Gruppe*, 7 *Jagdgeschwader*, from Parchim, dived onto the Americans as they headed for home and shot down eight Flying Fortresses and five escort fighters. With a further 16 four-engined machines going down to AA, this amounted to another local success for Home Air Defence. But for the enemy it meant a loss rate of barely 2%, and at this stage of the war the Americans would not lose much sleep over the loss of 24 bombers out of 1,200.

On the German side, two Me262s were lost, 26 *Jagdgeschwader* lost two pilots that day and I *Gruppe*, 2 *Jagdgeschwader*, reported three killed.

* In his book 'The First and the Last'. (Author)

On the following day US 8th Air Force was joined by RAF Bomber Command over West Germany, and the enemy fighters were able to pin down the German defence so thoroughly that they never looked like getting through to the bombers.

Both British 2nd TAF's Spitfires and American fighters in strength put in low-level attacks on German fighter airfields. 27 *Jagdgeschwader*, which at the time was just in the process of redeploying to the new airfields south of the Teutoburger Wald, suffered severely at their hands. For IV *Gruppe*, which had flown off from Achmer, March 19th proved to be the end of their existence as an operational unit. The Americans shot down virtually a whole *Staffel* over the Osnabrück area, killing six pilots and wounding five.

78th Fighter Group's Mustangs were on a ground-attack mission against the airfields between Rheine and Osnabrück. As they approached, they met between 40 and 50 machines from 26 and 27 *Jagdgeschwader*. The Americans went straight into the attack, catching some of the German formations while they were still climbing.

Their first victims were four of 26 *Jagdgeschwader's* 'long noses', which had already reached their tactical altitude. Three pilots were killed.

To the north of Osnabrück, IV *Gruppe*, 27 *Jagdgeschwader*, never really had a chance against the Mustangs. The Americans took on 14 *Staffel* over Wallenhorst and Hollage, and pursued them as far as the Wiehen Hills. The Americans claimed 32 kills but themselves lost five Mustangs.

Elements of I *Gruppe* took off about 1000 on their redeployment flight to Störmede, but a bunch of Spitfires from No 130 Squadron were on them in a flash. Flying low over the field, they caught some machines before they were even airborne. Two pilots, were shot down in flames, and one crash-landed in a wood.

Over the Brandenburg area the Mustangs accounted for two Me262s bringing the German fighter force's losses for March 19th to eight killed and seven wounded in air defence operations.

Sunday March 24th, 1945
With the cutting to pieces of 301 *Jagdgeschwader* at the beginning of the month 1 *Jagddivision* had already lost a substantial part of the force under its command, and on March 24th 300 *Jagdgeschwader* too suffered a decisive defeat. On this day US 8th Air Force put up a total of 1,400 bomber sorties in a major operation against a dozen or more Luftwaffe bases east of the Rhine, some in Holland and some in West Germany. These raids were carried out in support of the Allied airborne operations at Wesel, where Montgomery's British troops were about to cross the Rhine.

It was about noon when the Americans, flying low, swept across the countryside between the Teutoburger Wald and the Lippe to take on the airfields in that area. There can be no doubt that the destruction wrought on the German bases and the loss of hundreds of machines on the ground very severely impaired the German day and night fighter effort.

Over Störmede, where I *Gruppe*, 27 *Jagdgeschwader*, were based at this time, a major battle developed between a strong force of Mustangs and the Messerschmitts of I and III *Gruppen*. The unit had already been stretched to the limit, and now it lost another twelve pilots, four from I *Gruppe* and eight from III *Gruppe*. Over and above this, three pilots were wounded by machine-gun fire on the Störmede field.

A little later 300 *Jagdgeschwader's* turn came, just east of Göttingen. II *Gruppe* under the 24-year-old 1st Lieut Radener and small elements from I and IV *Gruppen* had flown west from Thuringia to be directed by ground control on to the reported American incursion. In a bitter action II *Gruppe*, the assault *Gruppe*, was completely wiped out, losing 20 of its Focke-Wulfs. 5 *Staffel* lost five pilots, though 6 *Staffel* simply ceased to exist; six of its pilots were killed in action. With 7 *Staffel* also losing two pilots, II *Gruppe*, casualties amounted to 14 killed and one wounded—a blow from which it was never to recover.

American losses on the other hand were negligible.

Now the German fighter force was well down the slope of its decline. Another six costly weeks of attrition were to go by before Germany finally collapsed, and a further 200 pilots were to lose their lives.

Fighter losses on March 24th, 1955

Units taking part	Killed/ missing	Wounded	Total pers/cas	Aircraft	Locality
III./JG7	3	3	6	Me262A	Grossen, Harz, Wittenberg
I./JG27	4	3	7	Me109 K-4	Osnabruck, Teutoburger Wald, Stormede
			16		
I.JG300	2		2	Me109 G-10	Gottingen, Lobnitz,
II./JG300	4	1	15	FW190 A-8/A-9	Kothen
IV./JG300	1	1	1	Me109 G-14	
			18		
Total losses	31	9	40		

(against incursions from the West and South)

Special Force Elbe

Saturday April 7th, 1945

As long as fuel and aircraft were available, the remnants of the fighter units battled on day by day. But then came that madcap enterprise known as 'Special Force Elbe', which delivered the knock-out punch to the fighter force. The originator of the 'Elbe' operation was Col Hajo Herrmann, who had already made a name for himself with other proposals, all of them controversial but not always to be dismissed out of hand. When for instance he was commanding 1/30 *Jagddivision* at the time of the Battle of Berlin, it was his idea to lift the blackout so that the RAF bombers with their dark camouflage would stand out against the bright background and offer the night-fighters a better target. There was no reason to suppose that a lit-up city would be bombed any less haphazardly than a blacked-out one.

But the formation of a 'ram unit', which from the very beginning took on the character of a suicide squad, produced a flood of objections; both Col Gollob, Director of Fighters, and the Inspector of Day Fighters, Col Dahl, turned it down. Despite this, and for reasons which can perhaps only be understood against the background of the situation at the time, 'Special Force Elbe' was set up at Stendal. Few members of it survived the day of April 7th, 1945, and their lips still remain sealed. This account must therefore confine itself to the facts.

Two days earlier, on April 5th, over 1,000 heavy bombers had flown in over Central and South Germany for heavy raids on Nuremberg and Plauen. Nineteen were shot down, but at the cost of 42 German machines. On the morning of April 7th 1,200 bombers and 800 fighters from US 8th Air Force were again headed for North Germany. From their bases near Stendal and Gardelegen 183* Focke-Wulfs and Messerschmitts of the Special Force scrambled, covered by a strong force of Me262 jet fighters from 7 *Jagdgeschwader* and 54 *Kampfgeschwader* (Fighters).

The pilots were briefed to close to point-blank range before opening fire, to come back with at least one kill on a heavy-bomber to their name and—if necessary—to destroy the enemy bomber by ramming it. No details are available of the units from which this Special Force was formed or how the pilots came to be selected for it. Certainly men from 300 and 301 *Jagdgeschwader* were among them.

It was a very cold morning on April 7th. Visibility was almost 10 miles and the sky was about three quarters overcast with cumulus. Up at 36,000 feet, the height from which the German fighters were to dive onto the Americans, it was about 20° below. The 'Elbe' fighters made a sighting over the south of Lüneburg Heath, Nienburg and the Steinhuder Meer. They drove their attack home hard; the Mustangs reacted vigorously but simply could not stop the German machines breaking through to the leading bomber formation. About 50 piston-engined fighters and a few Me262s reached the bomber spearhead. The Americans appeared to be taken by surprise at the strength of the fighter attack; they were on the receiving end of an operation that bore a certain resemblance to the Japanese *Kamikaze* tactics. A handful of Focke-Wulfs would come roaring in, pressing their attack home with complete disregard of danger; 452nd Bombardment Group lost two Flying Fortresses and 385th and 388th Bombardment Group one each. And a Messerschmitt accounted for a fifth B17 from 490th Bombardment Group.

The battle raged on for at least three quarters of an hour; the Me262s managed to account for one Flying Fortress each from 100th and 390th Bombardment Groups and an Me109 rammed a Liberator head on. It was a day of sacrifice for the Americans too.

But in the last analysis the outcome was horrifying and, predictably enough, fell far short of expectations. Only 15 German machines of those that took off returned to base. Seventy seven pilots were reported killed or missing; the rest had successfully taken to their parachutes. A pointless sacrifice. The German

---

* Other sources quote only 120. (Author)

side admitted 133 machines lost and claimed a total of 50 enemy aircraft shot down. Even if these figures were correct, they could have had no influence whatever on the course of the War. The Americans by contrast reported the destruction of 100 German aircraft, 59 of them by fighters, for a loss of only eight bombers.

One figure is probably too high, the other definitely too low. But what of it —what matters is that this desperate throw sent to their death over 75 young Germans, many of them fresh from the flying schools.

The proof that home air defence was now effectively at an end came on Thursday, April 10th, when a massive American raid went in on the jet fighter fields in North Germany. Briest, Burg, Oranienburg, Lärz and Parchim suffered extensive damage to installations and machines. This resulted in the move of the Me262 units to Czechoslovakia, where US 8th Air Force could no longer get at them. Meanwhile Hitler raged away at the Luftwaffe; he simply could not understand why the runways could not be restored overnight.

On Friday April 13th the Americans really began to take the Luftwaffe out on the ground. Thunderbolts from 56th Fighter Group destroyed 95 machines on North German airfields, including Eggebek in the northwest of Schleswig-Holstein. Three days later, on the following Monday, it was the turn of the South German fields, 353rd Fighter Group destroying some 110 aircraft on the ground. And 125 machines went up in smoke on airfields in the Sudetenland. The next day the Mustangs were back again to send another 200 aircraft up in flames. This sealed the fate of the Luftwaffe, and of the fighter force in particular.

The achievements of our gallant fighter pilots, their fearlessness and their resolve, must never be forgotten, least of all when the conditions under which they fought are borne in mind. It was perhaps best summed up in the words of an unknown fighter pilot, though even these hardly began to reflect the true measure of the tragedy:

'We were losing pilots all the time, and had to get used to seeing new faces and hearing new names. So now I can hardly recall a single name—things were all mixed up. Almost every day new pilots came up from the reinforcement units or the schools, full of hope and optimism. The quartermasters were reluctant to find billets for any more pilots; they hated to see these young men take the air when the grim routine of bringing back their remains had to be so often repeated.'

Now, or so we hope, those grim days are over. Our enemies of yesterday are now our friends. And long may it remain so, for a new Operation Baseplate must never happen and another Special Force Elbe must never come into being.

One Flight's Losses in Home Air Defence
(5 *Staffel*, 300 *Jagdgeschwader*, October 1944–March 1945)

In conclusion it would be well to review the casualties in a home-based assault *Staffel* over a period of only six months. 5 *Staffel*, 300 *Jagdgeschwader*, with its FW190 A-8s lost 19 pilots killed or missing and six wounded in this time, so that its aircrew virtually had to be replaced twice over. At the turn of the year, three *Staffel* leaders were killed within four weeks.

And this example does not stand alone. Other *Staffeln* had a similar story to tell, some of them an even sadder one.